his way...
o*r no way*

Paula Rivers
with **Maggie Allen**

Copyright © 2019 Maggie Allen

Published by PPR Publishing,
19 Kingswell Road, Northampton NN2 6QB

www.pprpublishing.co.uk

All rights reserved

This book is a work of non-fiction, a true story based on the experiences and recollections of the author. However, all names of individuals, dates and locations of events, and other identifiable characteristics have been changed to protect the privacy and identity of those concerned.

A CIP catalogue record for this book
is available from the British Library.

ISBN: 978 1 9164347 2 1

Printed and bound in Great Britain by IngramSpark /
Lightning Source UK Ltd.

Dedication

This book is dedicated to my beloved children, my loving parents and my darling Grandma.

I have written this, my true story, in the hope that it might help others who find themselves in abusive relationships and feel they are trapped, unable to escape, for whatever reason.

There is always a way out.
There is always a better life.
Believe me.

Acknowledgements

To my writer, Maggie Allen (The Write Word) – I will be forever grateful for her kind understanding and patience while writing this difficult story, and I will cherish Maggie for her great friendship and wisdom.

And to those amazing people who stood by me and helped me along the way, even when I tried my damnedest to conceal the truth, and in the face of danger to themselves. I am truly grateful to you all.

Foreword

A message from Paula's relatives, Gwen and Simon

Having known Paula from her early childhood, we were quite concerned when she announced her impending marriage to John. Something wasn't right, and we both had a very strong gut feeling about him. Of course, we hoped we were completely wrong and so decided not to say anything to her. It wasn't our place to interfere.

Paula had had a very secure and loving upbringing until things fell apart when she was just 13, when her mother died suddenly and unexpectedly.

John was a most impatient man, who always seemed distant and aloof. He made it quite clear that he was never happy to see us, or indeed any of Paula's family. We were made to feel unwelcome at their home, and even our phone calls to her were cut short in a most aggressive manner, which was totally uncalled for – all we were doing was keeping in touch, like a normal family. At first, we were worried, but we later became terrified of John. We did feel for Paula but felt powerless to do anything. The situation, as we were seeing it, upset us greatly.

Paula didn't have to tell us about her problems with John – *we just knew*. It's always easier to see clearly when you're looking in from the outside. There was no hiding the truth. Almost from the very start, he controlled her in so many ways and soon had her cut off from all her family members; she had no choice but to see family and friends in total secret, including us.

It was very sad to witness this, after all that had happened earlier in her life. But Paula was determined to make the marriage work and give her children a happy, stable home, just as she'd had. Whenever we did manage to see her, she appeared terribly drawn and on edge, as if she wasn't able to be herself. We just supported her as best we could through those years.

When the marriage was finally over, Paula began to look very different: gone was that constant stress and she was like someone who'd had a huge weight lifted from their shoulders. Of course, everything came tumbling out, the hideous truth that we had already guessed at years ago. It was awful to hear and it made us weep – even Simon cried.

Seeing Paula rebuild her life, day by day, and eventually find happiness, has been inspirational and her story offers hope to others who might find themselves in any similar situation.

Foreword

A message from Paula's close friend, Kate

I first met my lovely friend, Paula, at nursery when our children were very young. With baby Alice in her pram, Paula was dropping 3-year-old David off. My little girl was the same age as him and I also had a baby in tow!

We bonded instantly and we would laugh together and cry together over what hard work it all was, and we'd joke about our 'good old days' when we could have a lie-in! With regular get-togethers, our friendship blossomed and I knew Paula was the one good friend I could count on. Sensible, kind, funny, and a great confidante: I had no doubt that she never repeated anything I had entrusted her with.

Of course, now it turns out that she was a bit *too good* at keeping quiet – I never knew the truth about John for many years. Paula kept it all to herself, which proves the level of her commitment and determination to try to resolve the situation. She didn't want her secret to get out, which nobody can blame her for, but it does upset me that she couldn't confide in me sooner than she did. It must have been a huge burden for all of that time.

When I first saw bruises on her arms, I was really shocked, but Paula tried to make excuses and pass it off as nothing – but eventually she broke down and told me the truth.

That fateful morning of Alice's eighteenth birthday when Paula rang me, I was still in my pyjamas. She sounded so distressed, I knew something really bad had happened, which was odd because I'd just been wondering how the special day was going, knowing how much effort Paula had put into preparing everything. I thought, surely John hadn't kicked off today of all days – and so early in the morning? That would be unforgivable.

Throwing a coat on to cover my nightwear, I was at Paula's place in about five minutes, because I realised it must be serious, whatever had happened. What greeted me was a scene of utter destruction, and undeniable family breakdown. Paula was sobbing as if her heart would break. I just hugged her and held on to her.

The floor was littered with broken dog bowls and dog food, there was water everywhere, wrapping paper and destroyed gifts were scattered around between the lounge and the kitchen. The settees and coffee table were all out of place and a table lamp lay on its side on the floor. There was total silence, apart from Paula weeping.

I had arrived shortly after a violent struggle

between John and poor Alice. Paula had finally told John to leave, and he had gone only minutes before I got there. He was to be dealt with by the law now, not before time. Alice had left in a taxi, in tears, her young heart broken and her future memories of her eighteenth birthday forever blighted. David was upstairs in his room, in shock.

That was the day when Paula's marriage finally ended. John had crossed the line: being violent towards the children was Paula's boundary, beyond which *nothing* was acceptable. We all have a line like that. I knew by the state of the place and the atmosphere that there would be no going back: what John had just done was, indeed, the final straw.

I have always been a great believer in marriage, but sometimes it really needs to end.

It's a great relief to me that Paula has finally gained control of her life and can now live without fear. Nobody should have to live a life of intimidation, bullying and abuse. She has set both herself and her children free, and that, to me, is wonderful to witness.

Paula, my dearest friend, I will always be here for you and I know you are always here for me, too. You are a true inspiration and a guiding light to others.

Introduction

Until death us do part...
And that's very nearly how it was, for Paula.

This is the true-life story of a young woman who married the wrong man. When she started to notice signs that perhaps he wasn't the most stable person in the world, she made excuses for him – he was stressed about business, he had a lot on his mind, he needed a break, he was tired, etc, etc.

And, when things got much worse and he became violent and abusive towards her, she constantly forgave him, gave him the benefit of the doubt, and believed his endless promises that things would be better from now on. She believed beyond doubt that he would change, that it wouldn't happen again. But he didn't, and it did.

He was incapable of changing – in fact, he didn't see there was anything wrong with him, or with how he was behaving, so why should he have to change? According to him, it was Paula who was causing all of their problems, *she* was the troubled one, *she* was the unstable one. So he never changed, he just became more angry, more aggressive, more violent and abusive. Time and time again, and much, much worse.

When a passive person is in a coercively controlling relationship and the abusive partner constantly blames the other person, constantly accuses that person of wrongdoing, and constantly reinforces that everything bad that happens is the other person's fault, the abused person can easily begin to doubt him/herself, and Paula did just that.

She spent a lot of time trying to work out where *she* was going wrong, and what *she* could possibly do to try to resolve the situation. She tried all of the obvious things – cooking his favourite meals, dressing in clothes he particularly liked, staying out of his way whenever he seemed more likely to explode, agreeing with his opinions and ideas... but nothing worked, because nothing *could have worked*. And, because her efforts fell on stony ground, she felt she was even more of a failure, she lost even more of her confidence and she doubted herself as a wife, a mother, and a human being. Unfortunately, this is a very common trait of this type of relationship.

The problem with Paula's marriage was that she was a gentle soul, kind and thoughtful, generous and considerate, raised by a family who taught her honesty, decency and strong moral values. In itself, of course, her admirable character is a good, positive thing, but when put together with someone who needed to have a victim, a person to control, to bully, to demean and abuse, the lovely Paula didn't stand a chance.

It's so easy, looking in from the outside, to say, "Why didn't you just leave?" And some people even go as far as to almost blame Paula for her unhappy circumstances, "You must have known it was never going to work – you were just making it worse by staying!" But leaving isn't always easy, as Paula found out.

She would be threatened, her family were threatened, the children were threatened – this man knew no boundaries. "If you try to leave again, I'll kill your family and you'll meet with a very nasty accident." He would tell her that the children would be taken from her because he could "prove she was an unfit mother", and Paula couldn't bear the idea of her beautiful son and daughter having to stay with him if anything happened to her.

It was all about control, and John had all of it.

People often use the term 'gutted' to describe how they feel when something tragic happens to them, something that knocks them sideways, something too dreadful for words. I suppose because it means feeling like your insides are being torn out.

…................

Although not a word I would normally use, there was one day in all of the years of our messed-up lives when that one word could possibly best explain how I felt.

The children were, by this time, totally aware that our situation at home could only be described as 'living on a knife edge', not daring to fall either way because there would be no good way to fall.

They knew that there was no way we could ever tell if their father would arrive home in a good mood and be happy, playful Daddy – or if he would be the angry monster we all feared. This applied whether he'd been at work, at the pub, at his mother's or anywhere else. They said Daddy was "sometimes nice" and "sometimes nasty".

As much as I tried my utmost to make their lives as happy, stable and fun-filled as possible, they weren't stupid. They knew how things were.

One day, when Alice had gone to school and I went into her room to clean, I found a diary on her bed – something she'd never done before, as she normally took that diary wherever she went.

Of course, I couldn't resist having a peep inside – knowing this was wrong and feeling bad about doing it, but I just had to, especially given our circumstances.

I was horrified. Yes – gutted.

My seven-year-old daughter had drawn a giant monster, with long arms and very big teeth. He was coloured in with red crayon and I could tell her work had been done with great determination and emotion, because the paper was almost torn through in places. Above the monster was one single word. 'Dad'.

There was another picture, this one was clearly me, lying on the settee with a wine glass (oh, dear God, is this how my child sees me?) and I was obviously crying. The face on the 'me' in the picture was very sad.

It was heartbreaking.

I turned the page and there was 'A Dad diary', where Alice had kept a record over the weeks of her dad's moods each day. She noted just one word for each of the entries, either 'good' or 'bad'. There were very few good days, many bad ones and even a couple marked 'very bad'. She had also written in her own words a sort of summing-up:

> My dreams have never been successful, so I long that dad would be kinder to mum, its awful what he has done. So I hope its ok now (the future). I am the past.
> Alice x

To see this written in her own handwriting broke my heart. And yet, I still couldn't see a way out of the hell we were living in.

....

There are so many – too many – examples of domestic abuse incidents resulting in extremely tragic circumstances, the worst of which culminate in the death of a partner, and sometimes, sadly, in the death of a child or children. Such a waste of life.

A great number of these cases cite a glaring lack of adequate response or support, whether that's from the law, from the medical professionals, mental health services, or whatever else. One such case made headlines in the UK and eventually brought about big changes in the way the system works.

Clare Wood, 36, mother of a 10-year-old daughter, divorced and lonely, met a man via the internet. He was George Appleton, aged 40, a fairground worker from the Traveller community. The couple got together in April 2007.

Although neither Clare's father nor her brother could take to the new boyfriend, the relationship appeared to be going well, and, seeing how happy she was, Clare's father, Michael, tried his best to be supportive, even when the pair started discussing marriage. He was relieved, however, when Clare told him she had finished with Appleton in October 2008.

Clare confided to Michael that Appleton was making a nuisance of himself, seemingly unable or unwilling to accept that the relationship was over, and, worried for her safety, Michael asked her to move back to West Yorkshire to be with him. Clare didn't want to uproot her little girl, and she tried to reassure her father that the situation was under control.

In February 2009, Michael was trying to contact Clare and couldn't reach her, making him extremely concerned, so he asked her ex-husband, father of Clare's daughter, to check on her at her home.

On entering the house, he discovered Clare's dead body, cruelly beaten and burnt. She had been strangled and then set on fire.

Following an intense national manhunt over six days, Appleton was found. He had hanged himself in a derelict pub, ending his own life.

Michael found out that the criminal record Clare had mentioned Appleton had, concerning motoring offences, was actually a record of imprisonment on two separate occasions for convictions of harassment and assaults on women, including one for kidnapping an ex-girlfriend.

It transpired that Clare had complained on several occasions to Greater Manchester Police about Appleton's behaviour following her ending the relationship, her allegations covering criminal damage, harassment, death threats and attempted rape.

Michael began asking questions. Why hadn't Clare been given appropriate support when she made these complaints? More to the point, why had she not been advised of Appleton's criminal past?

The grieving father set out on a mission to spread the word about these failings in the system and to get something done to protect innocent partners of violent and abusive people, and his cause was picked up by a Manchester radio station's chief reporter. Michael fought over the following years, compiling evidence, circulating petitions and drumming up support from the media, from politicians and others who saw the sense of his campaign.

Following Michael's testimony at the inquest in 2011 into his daughter's death, the Coroner, Jennifer Leeming, concluded that a woman in an abusive relationship should have the right to find out about her partner's violent past.

After four years of Michael's tireless work, Theresa May, who was Home Secretary at the time, took the campaign to public consultation and the scheme was launched in four police areas initially. Then, on International Women's Day, the eighth of March 2014, *Clare's Law* was officially rolled out across England and Wales.

Formally known as the *Domestic Violence Disclosure Scheme*, it allows police forces to reveal details of a person's history of domestic violence or other acts of violence, to their partner – or a friend or relative can apply and they will receive the information.

All it takes is a formal application.

In the first ten months of its existence, an average of five women each day were being given information revealing whether or not their partners had a past record of abusive or violent behaviour. *Clare's Law* was pronounced a resounding success.

For Michael Brown, Clare's father, although this was a wonderful result and something to be immensely proud of, how sad that this wasn't in place when his lovely daughter needed it.

…..…………….

Paula's true story is an illustration of the human condition laid bare, and it touches on aspects such as

Stockholm Syndrome[1], the psychology of victims identifying and empathising with their abuser in what is termed an act of self-preservation, albeit carried out on an unconscious level.

Paula has written her story in the hope that it might help other people who find themselves in similar circumstances. We all know it happens, and there are some very frightening statistics on domestic violence and abuse.

In the year ending March 2017, the police recorded a total of 1.1 million domestic abuse-related crimes and incidents, with almost 50% of these being registered as crimes. This figure accounts for almost one third of the total number of crimes and violence in England and Wales. [Office for National Statistics]

Even sadder than those figures is the knowledge that many more cases of domestic violence and abuse go unreported.

What Paula's story tells us is that there is always a way out, there is always an option, and **you can break free**, *no matter what.*

If you are in a relationship with someone who doesn't respect you, who bullies and hurts you,

---

[1] *Stockholm Syndrome:* Term coined by criminologist Nils Bejerot to describe a situation where hostages bonded with their captors during a bank robbery in Stockholm, Sweden, in 1973

someone who controls you and makes you feel afraid and alone in the world – there is only one answer. You need to get away from that person, whatever it takes.

This book tells Paula's true story as it happened, with only the names of people and places changed to protect those involved.

Chapter 1: Alice's 18th Birthday

How wonderful! My daughter's eighteenth birthday. It was going to be the most special day, I would make sure of that. Memorable. Well, that day certainly turned out to be one we would remember – but not in a good way. Not good at all.

No matter what, I had always loved being a mother, and this approaching milestone brought a surge of pride as I allowed myself to enjoy the idea that both of my children were adults now, both equipped and able to survive, to take care of themselves and each other, should anything happen to me and their father. As I considered this new phase of our family life, I realised this was what I had been working towards, and this was going to be a turning point for us all. It made me happy just to know that my son and daughter would not need to be looked after by members of the family: for years now, relatives on both sides had proved to be a contentious area of our lives and I welcomed this new situation with open arms. So, for many different reasons, this day would be even more special, a cause for true celebration, a very happy day.

The week or so leading up to the birthday had been, shall we say, turbulent. But that was nothing new. I had hoped that John, my husband and father of our children, would manage to latch on to the enjoyment, the fun, the excitement of the upcoming family festivity. As always, I was kidding myself. John didn't do 'fun', he didn't want to take part in anything I did with the children purely for enjoyment, and – the really sad part – he didn't even see his own offspring as a reason to be happy, something to celebrate. As the special day grew closer, he remained his normal belligerent, angry, abrasive self and I remained the object of his vile behaviour. His actions towards me were vicious: instead of speaking to me, he would spit out words with such venom, they hurt me like knives through my flesh.

"What are you doing?" he snarled at me as I was getting the house ready for the big day, "pissing about with this trivial crap – why don't you do something useful?" And off he stormed, back to his office.

He was always knocking me, belittling me, whatever I did. All I ever got was his utter contempt, making me feel like I was nothing, like an annoying fly that should be swatted because it had no purpose, because it was just *there*. And yet, I still had to keep the family together, even though our own family meant nothing to him. The only thing that mattered to him was himself, his own existence – and his business, of course. He was so wrapped up in his work, it was as if he and it became one and the same thing.

I was hanging some decorations in the hallway, all bright, brilliant and colourful, still determined to make this occasion as happy and as much fun as I could. As I took hold of a chair to stand on so I could reach up higher, a sudden sharp pain stabbed deep inside my knee and I buckled. A burning shockwave bolted down into my calf muscle. *God! That hurts!* I caught my breath and glanced down at the black and purple bruising on my leg. I know some people would think that constantly being bruised was appalling, but for me it was nothing out of the ordinary, just normal life. By now, I'd had years of the beatings and bruising, and I was used to it. According to John, it was my fault because "You bruise too easily, you stupid fat cow." How distorted was his thinking, to accuse me of being at fault, when it was *his* fists and *his* vicious kicks that caused the bruises? This particular week, I even had bruise marks on my breasts from when he had kicked me for some reason while I was picking up the dog bowl. I remembered how that had knocked the wind out of me, but I couldn't remember why he had done it. There was usually no real reason… I stretched my leggings down to cover the marks and got on with my decorating.

What hurts me the most is that the children were every bit as used to his dreadful behaviour as I was. They saw his destruction of our family life as an everyday occurrence – it was simply how things were, just normal. I really hate myself for that.

The birthday arrived. The instant I was awake, I was mentally running through the plans for Alice's weekend of partying and celebration. It was still quite early and I was pleasantly surprised to see a smiling David, my boy, wander into the kitchen not long after me. I poured him some of the fresh coffee I'd just made and slowly took a deep breath, enjoying one of those small things in life that make so much difference – the aroma of fresh coffee making the house feel cosy and calm first thing in the morning. Making it feel almost *normal*.

We sat together, both excited at the prospect of the day ahead for our third Musketeer. That's how we were, the three of us. I opened the fridge door and took out a big white box, placing it carefully on the breakfast bar, lifting the lid so that David could see the birthday cake I'd had made – the top was decorated with tiny handbags and high-heeled shoes, and dotted around between them were little sign-posts with names of exotic far-away places that Alice would love to visit, like Nepal, Marrakesh and Antigua, all made in brightly coloured sugar paste and icing. Delightful.

We heard Alice moving around upstairs, then the shower running. Thankfully, John was still asleep in his room, where I hoped he would remain until Alice's boyfriend arrived to whisk her away for the day. At least then she could be spared having to witness – or be a part of – her father's usual inappropriate antics, and she and Andrew could go off to enjoy whatever he had planned for her.

Obviously, I was asking for too much.

Alice appeared, beautiful in her new powder blue dress, her shoulder-length blonde hair lightly curled and her make-up perfect – so lovely, and I was bursting with pride. She held her arms out and the three of us hugged for a few precious moments.

I'd bought some really expensive champagne so she could have her first official (and legal!) drink while she opened her gifts. Then, when she had torn open every piece of pretty wrapping, I'd watch her face as we presented her with our special gift. I'd wanted to get her something different and unique that she would treasure. She had always loved her birthstone, the delicately coloured aquamarine, and I'd managed to find a jeweller who made pendants to order. I chose her initial, the letter A, as the frame, made in filigree silver, and in the centre was the most beautiful pale blue stone. I knew she'd love it.

As John was showing no signs of getting up to join us, I decided to give Alice her gift now, so that she could slip away the moment Andrew arrived and still have her gift with her all day. She opened the shiny black box and gasped, her eyes wide with delight. David carefully fastened the chain around his sister's neck and we all stood there, just admiring it, as Alice kept modelling her new necklace in the mirror, all the while thanking me for doing something so thoughtful for her.

Standing there with my two amazing children, I kept asking myself, "Why can't life be like this all the time?"

I was smiling, but inside I was praying that Andrew would ring the doorbell now, right now – please, God, *make it now!* But before Andrew arrived, that special day turned into the worst possible nightmare.

Suddenly, we heard John stirring upstairs. His voice made us all jump at the same time. "Alice, where's my birthday girl? Come here and let me say happy birthday before you go!" Simple words, and if they had been spoken by anyone else, they would have sounded harmless, even affectionate... but they seemed like the harshest, most cruel and depraved threat any human could possibly utter. Alice and I exchanged a quick glance. She knew my smile was fake but she smiled back anyway. The pressure now was to try to stall John, to stop him coming downstairs yet, because he would just kick off about Andrew, what a 'waste of space' he was, how his family were all 'peasants', that Alice was wasting her time and ruining her life with 'that prat' and so on. Or he'd have a go about the gifts I'd bought her, telling us they were 'rubbish', an 'absolute load of crap' and a 'waste of my hard-earned cash'... or maybe worse than that.

Alice called up the stairs, as calmly as she could, "OK, Dad, just let me finish opening a few presents then I'll be with you." But whatever she had said wouldn't have made any difference: John was suddenly thudding along the landing and hurtling down the stairs as if the devil were after him. His angry words reached us in a full-on attack. "Alice! Has your brain-dead boyfriend arrived yet? Where's he taking you? A trip to

La-la Land? Ha-ha! He's such a pleb, no way am I letting you go off with him!" Then he glared at the opened gifts among the gaily-coloured wrapping paper on the rug. "And what's all this tat?" His head jolted round to face me as he continued to rant – just as we'd known he would – and I actually felt his spit on my cheek. No matter how many times someone spits at you, it's always just as much an insult as the first time. And, with John, being spat on had become a regular occurrence for me.

My heart was pounding now, my head throbbing, as I stood there, unable to move, too frightened to react in any way. "Look at you!" He was on a roll now and he was winding himself up to the inevitable.

"You're a bloody disgrace, woman! Letting our daughter have anything to do with that peasant! Call yourself a mother?"

As he hurled these insults towards me, he was moving closer and his right arm started to rise in front of me. I closed my eyes and waited for the attack.

There was a sudden loud crash very close to where I was standing. It shocked me into opening my eyes and I saw John stooped over in a defensive position, his hands clutching his head, as a trickle of blood eased its way through his fingers. There were pieces of a heavy pottery bowl strewn around the floor.

"You little bitch!" He sprang towards Alice and, before either of us could move, his clenched fist landed with full force on the side of her head. She screamed, her eyes ablaze, perhaps with the pent-up anger and all sorts of emotions from the years of torment he had put us through. She launched herself at him and I was now witnessing a fight, a brawl, between father and daughter. It was horrible – shouting, swearing, fists flying and feet kicking, two people thrashing and flailing around, and I was terrified because someone was going to be really hurt – or maybe even worse.

Where was David? He was up in his room playing his music so he wouldn't be able to hear the uproar. I was completely helpless, unable to move or do anything. I just stood there, frozen with fear. Enraged even more, John let Alice go, turned and lashed out at me, shouting yet more insults and abuse.

"You're so thick! You are useless! You're not normal – you need help, you do! Everyone knows it."

I darted for the stairs, my plan to get to David so that, at least, the three of us could put up some sort of defence against John's onslaught. He was by now completely beside himself, purple-faced and raving. I didn't make it. A hand grabbed my arm, twisted me sideways and I was thrown down on to the bottom stairs, then a vicious kick landed right where my latest bruises had only just come out. The renewed pain was accompanied by more screamed verbal abuse, but I wasn't listening any longer.

The whole scene was utter carnage. Poor Alice – I desperately wanted to comfort her, to make it all right, but she was sobbing, shouting at John to leave us alone, to stop being such a bully… but he would never accept that any of this was down to him. It was my fault, everything bad was always my fault.

John landed another kick to my thigh and then stooped over me, his contorted face almost touching my hair as I tried to turn away, He cleared his throat in a ridiculously exaggerated way and then, in a final gesture of his contempt, he spat right in my eye, a big glob of slimy sputum. It was disgusting, sickening. Jamming his foot down on my neck as he ran past me up the stairs two at a time, he was calling out to David as he went, "Look what your stupid mother's gone and done now! She's ruined Alice's birthday! Bloody mental, she is!"

Alice helped me to my feet and we almost crawled up to her room. Poor girl, she looked such a mess now – torn dress, hair all over the place, make-up smeared, tear-stained face and now with a swelling starting to show on her cheek. With John back in his room, still chuntering away, we somehow managed to get her cleaned up and into a different outfit, hair tidy and some light make-up that hopefully wouldn't draw attention to the injury.

I was so tempted to ring the police but this was my daughter's coming-of-age birthday and having the police turn up, and all that would follow, would only make the day even more of a disaster – if that were possible.

But I was acutely aware that Andrew really would be arriving any minute now, and with John still there and in this rage the poor lad would be in danger. I was racking my brain for some way of avoiding this potential problem, and then everything changed. I heard John talking to someone, presumably on his mobile, and he was chatting away, normal as could be, laughing and joking with whoever was on the other end. Talk about Jekyll and Hyde. The chatting ended and John dashed downstairs and out of the house, yelling over his shoulder, "Make sure you're in a better mood when I get back."

I know I said "Thank you, God" out loud. I was a crumpled, battered heap, but at least now we were all spared for a while, and Andrew would be safe. Somehow, I pulled myself together and went to tell David what had been going on. He hugged me but he didn't say anything. The doorbell rang. It was Andrew and I knew he could tell just from seeing me that things had kicked off again. He wasn't surprised, just sad. I saw the two of them off for their day together and hoped they could enjoy themselves, but I knew nothing could mend what had just been broken. I lay on the settee, shattered and unable to think straight – or think at all. I asked myself, how the hell had I allowed it to get to this, to become this bad? But I had no answer. I sobbed silently, then I cried aloud, unimaginable sadness pouring from somewhere deep inside me. I felt utter disbelief at how desperate the situation was. I ached so much, both in body and mind – and the worst ache of all was in my heart, for my children. David popped his head round the door to tell me he was going out, but I didn't ask where or for how long. I knew he needed to escape.

Eventually, I picked up the phone and rang my closest friend, Kate, the one person I could talk to. She was the one I'd always turned to when I needed to confide in someone about John's violence and the way things were. She came round straight away and we talked, quietly and calmly. We wept together when I told her how Alice's birthday had been ruined. This was without doubt the saddest day of my life, and of Alice's and David's, too. It was all so heartbreaking, and I can never forgive myself for that.

But something good did come out of that awful day. I knew it had to be the turning point for me and the children.

....

On that very same day, John was charged with GBH and a court injunction was issued against him. I was granted a Non-Molestation order and an Occupation order. He must not come to the house for a period of twelve months, under threat of being arrested. This was real, it was happening – and this would be the final time.

Later in the evening when Alice came home after her day out, she stood in front of me and I saw a young woman who was weighted down with a burden that had become far too heavy, and I knew she could take no more. She spoke, her voice flat, without emotion. "I can't do this, Mum. It has to end. It's me or my Dad. You choose." She turned and went up to her room.

Maybe I had needed to hear it from her or David,

but when she said it out loud, I knew that was it. We couldn't go on like this, or one of us would end up dead – or maybe in prison for murder. Either way, the future wasn't going to be any different from that horrendous day unless I changed it. So I did, even though in the end the decision had been made for me by my own daughter.

John had finally crossed the line. Attacking our daughter, our beautiful girl, instead of me, was what made the difference.

So, now this dreadful mess would be in the hands of the courts and the lawyers, and he wouldn't be able to wriggle out of anything from this point forward. This had to be our chance to get him out of our lives – permanently.

But, if I had imagined for one second that this would be the end of it, I was terribly mistaken...

....

I'd taken out court orders before, and always dropped the charges and cancelled the orders. Because *he* always convinced me it was the only way for all of us.

"OK, so I go to prison," he'd say sarcastically, "then what? You really need to think this through. No more business, so there'll be no money, you and the kids would have to change your lifestyle drastically. No big house, no fancy clothes, no nice car, no holidays, tuition fees... is that what you want for your children? Could you *really* live like that? I don't think so!"

And it wasn't just the material things – I'm certainly not that pathetic. The threat was much more than losing our comfortable life. John told me in words of one syllable that, if I did pursue the case against him and he was given a prison sentence, he would make certain that I had 'a little accident'. I had no doubt that he could organise such a fate for me if he chose: after all, there are people who do these things for a wad of cash. I simply couldn't consider the children being left without both parents – one dead and the other in prison. What sort of chance would they have? It didn't bear thinking about. So I didn't. I always gave in.

But this time the order stayed firmly in place for the twelve months. Both Alice and David started to settle down, to appear happier, and they didn't see their father for quite some time after that fateful day. All three of us were referred to a counsellor by our GP because she said we all showed signs of dangerously high-level stress and anxiety. We went for counselling sessions and I was prescribed anti-depressants which helped a bit, and, slowly but surely, we all began to leave behind that dreadful life. The control, the fear, the violence, constantly living on a knife-edge, terrified of falling either way.

I hated knowing how damaged my children were. I hated John for being the cause, and I hated myself even more for allowing it to happen and not doing something about it sooner. I blamed myself, even though David and Alice were both incredibly understanding. I was still the parent, the adult, the one who should have taken charge.

As for that beautiful special gift, the necklace that was to represent our family's love throughout Alice's life, she had worn it for about half an hour before all hell broke loose. It never saw the light of day again.

But we did.

Chapter 2: My Childhood

A three-bedroom semi in the suburbs with a big privet-hedged garden where we played on our swing for hours on end. We being me, my older sister and baby brother. Completing the picture, Mum and Dad and our lovely little Grandma.

She was Mum's mum, widowed when I was about seven, but definitely the best grandmother in the world and always in our lives, especially since she lived over the road. Dad's parents lived further away and had other grandchildren so we didn't see as much of them, but our special Grandma was all we needed; she was bright and feisty, and very much a part of our family life.

Dad grew vegetables in the garden, and just saying that reminds me of picking runner beans for Sunday lunch, or cutting up sticks of rhubarb when Mum was making a crumble for pudding.

Life was simple and we were happy. Isn't that how

family life should be? I can honestly say I never once heard Mum and Dad argue – something we children more than made up for, with our constant squabbling! And it was clear to everyone that they loved each other and shared a great mutual respect. A normal family. They say there's no such thing, but maybe our family was as near 'normal' as it gets.

In the 1960s, everyday existence was a lot more personal – more human – than today's computer-driven world where we order goods from unknown places, we pay money to unknown people and then we just hope that when the delivery van turns up, it will be with the actual item we wanted. Back then, we had real people who would come to the house and they would smile and chat and wave cheerio when they left.

There was the pop man with his bottles of fizzy drinks; the egg lady who kept hens that clucked and pecked in the sunshine and slept in their own little house; the fish man on Tuesdays and Fridays; the milkman in his white coat, carrying glass bottles of milk with yellow cream on top... We had a paper boy, an ice cream man whose brilliantly coloured van played tinkling music to let us know he was there, the Spot the Ball man, the deli man, and probably more.

As well as our happy little family unit, we had aunts, uncles and cousins who all featured regularly throughout our childhood. There was always so much fun to be had in summertime with our cousins and the neighbours' children, playing in a big shiny paddling pool on the lawn. Happy days.

But even the happiest families have their tragedies. Ours hit us when my sister, Megan, was just three years old. She was diagnosed with a retinoblastoma, a very rare form of cancer of the eye that affects children under the age of five. She had to have her right eye removed and I was told much later that Grandma had offered to give Megan one of her own eyes. It must have been a terribly sad and stressful time for everyone, and of course Megan was the centre of attention and the subject of much prayer.

Following her surgery and convalescence, she became more demanding, always appearing unsettled and petulant, to the point of throwing tantrums at times. In her later years she did suffer from some mental health issues, and this was attributed to the serious medical problem when she had been so very young.

Even when faced with such a trying time, all I know is that the family stuck together, pulled together and got through. Because that's how it should be, no matter what.

Because Mum and Dad both went out to work, Grandma was always there to do whatever was needed, like cooking lunch for us and walking us to school, so the ideal of a real family was a very obvious and strong presence in our young lives. I believe another reason for Grandma's constant support was that Mum had suffered from post-natal depression after I was born and she did occasionally have problems 'with her nerves'.

Something else that was part of our family life back

then was the church. And not just us, but many other families, lots of ordinary people, went to church every Sunday.

Don't get me wrong, I'm not talking about the strangely pious sackcloth-and-ashes folk, poring over their bibles and declaring pestilence and destruction on the non-repentant – no, just your average Mr and Mrs plus offspring, going to church once a week to listen to the service, sing a few hymns and leave feeling good about themselves and each other. The singing was always the best part for me: so many voices joined together in declaring a shared message about life, about love, about family.

There was, however, one awkward aspect of our weekly attendance at church. We would all get dressed up in our 'Sunday best' and very often some family matter or other would crop up and have to be dealt with, which meant arriving at church after the service had started, in turn resulting in us being paraded right down the aisle to the very front pews. I hated that, and I would imagine the people up in the gallery looking down on us, thinking how awful we were for daring to interrupt the minister.

I'm convinced this is when I began to develop a bit of a complex about people in authority, and I turned into a shy child who would do anything to avoid attracting attention. It became so bad, I wouldn't even call out in class when the teacher was taking the register! That sounds silly now, I know, but it was very real to me at the time.

So, Sundays were family days when we all dressed up in our finery to take a pew in the beautiful and imposing Evangelical church, and everyone would sing their hearts out so powerfully it felt like the roof might lift off at any moment! The minister would preach to us about heaven, about salvation, and about the importance of building a strong family, with the head of the house being, of course, the husband.

"For the husband is the head of the wife as Christ is the head of the Church." Ephesians 5:23

It's fair to say that the influence of the church in my childhood did shape my character in certain ways, but, unfortunately, it was more from the fear and being in awe of the whole church experience, and being made to feel extremely self-conscious. What I took from my time at church was the knowledge that you must always be 'on show', visible to everyone and therefore open to their criticism and judgement. So I learned that it was all about how you *appeared* to others, how people saw you, not how you felt inside yourself. In later years, this would definitely come back to bite me, when I felt it was vital to keep up appearances, rather than admit things were wrong and do something about it.

Church aside, I was a happy child who did well at school in all of my subjects, and I always had one special 'best friend', although I never got involved with any groups. Having one close friend suited my shy nature and my need for privacy.

Basically, I think we can all agree that it's impossible for any family to say things were 'normal', but I always felt I had a stable and generally happy upbringing.

Chapter 3: End of My Childhood

"Your mum's gone to be with Jesus."

It was the summer of 1978 and we'd been out, all of us together as a family, because it was such a lovely sunny day. The country park was a good few miles away and a bit of a bike ride but we loved it there, dodging the streams and jumping on and off the stepping-stones that together formed a meandering path across the cool, trickling water.

Full of childhood energy, we ran around in the bracken and climbed over the rocks, and then enjoyed the treat of delicious ice-creams while we rested and cooled down in the shade. The hot day had attracted quite a lot of families, mums and dads and children, all laughing together and munching on their picnic goodies.

We left around four o'clock to cycle the eight miles or so back home and it was still really very warm so the ride was pretty exhausting. There was never much traffic in those days, so riding a pushbike on the main roads was quite safe, and we would follow behind Dad with Mum bringing up the rear, often trailing behind and having to stop for a rest and to catch her breath, which we would all grumble about and we'd call out to her impatiently to come on and hurry up!

By the time we arrived back at the house, Mum must have been really tired and there was a mention of having fish and chips for tea, but that idea was soon dismissed as Mum began preparing a meal for us. We were famished after our exertions from the cycling, the heat and our energetic games. It's funny how you remember some small details and I know we had salad with lots of sandwiches, then ice-cream for pudding and we finished off with some French fancy cakes, all iced in pretty colours. It was normal to round off a family meal with something sweet and it was a tradition Grandma had passed on to us.

We were still sitting at the table eating when Mum said she felt weary and so was going upstairs to have a lie-down for a while. This was nothing out of the ordinary because the medication she was on did make her tired sometimes, so we didn't think anything of it. The three of us were looking forward to playing outside with our friends for a while, seeing as there was no sign yet of the sunshine disappearing and it was still only around six o'clock.

Suddenly, Mum's voice came from upstairs, shouting for Dad. She sounded distressed and he dashed up to her straight away. He told me later that he found her turning blue and complaining of chest pains.

He called down to me to fetch Grandma and I shot over the road and banged on her door, calling to her, "Grandma! Come quick! Mum's not well!" She hurried out, slamming the door shut behind her, and we both raced back across to our house.

Grandma ran straight upstairs and I followed her. It was awful, something you never forget. Mum was lying sprawled over the bed, not moving and with her eyes closed, and she was very pale and her skin seemed strangely blue. I was scared. Grandma immediately took over, trying to bring Mum round by giving her mouth-to-mouth and thumping on her chest while she counted out loud, "One, two, three..." and it felt as though time was standing still in a place where nothing was real any more, like a bad dream that I would soon wake up from, then I'd tell Mum about it and she'd make it all go away. Now I was really terrified because I knew something was seriously wrong.

"Call an ambulance, Paula!" Dad's words almost screamed at me and that meant this was a truly desperate situation, so I flew downstairs and grabbed the phone in the hallway, my fingers trembling as I dialled 999. In the kitchen, Michael and Megan were crying. "Is Mum going to die?"

"Don't be silly – mums don't die!" That would be unheard of, wouldn't it? Everyone had a mum, they were always there.

We three decided to go into our 'den' under the stairs where it was quiet and dark. We huddled together and said prayers, asking God to save Mum and not let her die. From upstairs, we could hear a huge commotion: Grandma was screaming, a real scream of fear and disbelief and all sorts of dreadful feelings. In minutes, the ambulance men arrived and their hurrying boots were loud on the stairs above our heads, loud and urgent.

We were so scared, and we had to peek through a gap in the door to get a glimpse of what was going on. In no time at all, they were thundering back down, this time with Mum on a stretcher. Very quickly, they put her in the ambulance where many neighbours had gathered around to see what was happening.

Dad jumped into the back of the ambulance and the doors closed. It drove away with the lights flashing and bells ringing. It was so unreal and I could barely breathe, I was terrified. Grandma stayed at the house with us and there was total silence. After all that rushing and thudding and shouting and loud bells – nothing. You could hear the clock ticking; I wanted it to stop because I felt it was ticking away Mum's life.

No-one spoke a word. Megan decided to clean out the budgie's cage because Mum had been asking her all week to do it. Grandma was crying ever so quietly. I looked around the room, as if I needed to find some clues as to what was happening. Mum's things were everywhere, her slippers by the fireplace where she'd left them, a letter standing on the mantelpiece waiting to be posted, the address on the front in her handwriting. All very normal. She would be fine, she had to be.

It must have been about an hour later when Dad came home. We all voiced the same question, "Where's Mum?" Our eyes searched his face to find some explanation, some reason why this was happening.

"Your mum's gone to be with Jesus."

We couldn't believe what he was telling us, nor could we understand it.

"What? What do you mean? She can't be gone!" We were all three completely in shock, in confusion and in denial.

As we stood there, looking to Dad for some help, some sense to make of it all, Grandma suddenly let out a loud scream. "No!" And then she just wailed, the most awful sound, and she covered her face with both hands and rocked back and forth, all the time wailing so pitifully. And then we knew for certain that Dad's words were true; the family who had just that day been cycling together in the sunshine, laughing and eating ice-cream and sitting down to tea together, that family was now devastated. Mum really was gone.

When I went to bed that night, I hoped I would wake up the next morning to our normality, with Mum and Dad and all of us safe, just like before that terrible day. Then I started thinking, what if I didn't wake up? What if I died in my sleep, or what if Dad died in his sleep? I couldn't think straight, and I couldn't cry. There was just this numbness, as if I was stuck in limbo.

Mum died on Saturday. On Monday morning I went to school, just like nothing had happened.

Remember, in those days there was no counselling, no support or anything for bereaved children who had lost a parent or other loved one. You just had to get on with it. That was the old way, no mollycoddling, no soppy stuff – just cold, harsh reality.

I was a little late for registration and when I walked in, the teacher was explaining to the other kids that "Paula's mum died at the weekend, so please try to be gentle with her." Everyone stared at me and I felt I was different now. They had mums and I didn't.

That first week after losing Mum saw our household behaving perfectly normally, with the only difference being that we had visitors, family and friends who popped in to bring flowers and chocolates as a sign of their sympathy. We never spoke about that dreadful afternoon or what had happened to Mum, and we didn't cry. She was in Heaven now, wasn't she? So, no point moping and wailing all over the place now, because Mum was with Jesus and He was looking after her. She was an angel in God's garden, that's what we had to believe. Even so, and as nice as that garden sounded, I'd rather she was back with us.

I had so many questions. Questions I couldn't ask, questions that would never be answered. Why had this happened to *my* mum? What could she possibly have done wrong? Why did she have to die? Did this mean *we* were going to die, too? I couldn't ask anything because I didn't want to upset anyone. So I kept it all inside.

Someone, presumably with good intentions,

suggested to Dad that perhaps we children should be taken to the mortuary so that we could say our goodbyes to Mum. Maybe they thought that seeing her lifeless body and having to acknowledge the reality that she was indeed dead and gone, would magically enable us to let it all out, scream and shout and cry, because that's what people thought we should be doing. Whatever this person's idea was, we were thankfully saved from this dreadful fate when an aunt of ours saw us walking down the road and she asked Dad where he was taking us.

"To the mortuary to say goodbye to their mum." Dad was no doubt in shock and he really had no idea how to handle three grieving children: he was just going along with what other people were telling him. Luckily for us, the aunt's intervention rescued us from visiting the place where dead people were kept before burial and I'm pretty certain it would have been a traumatic experience anyway.

We were much better off remembering Mum as we saw her on that last happy day in the sunshine. Not as a dead body, a lifeless corpse after a massive heart attack.

In the week leading up to the funeral, Dad cried a lot. He admitted to Grandma that he was feeling lonely and he was scared at the prospect of trying to raise the three of us on his own. He was talking about getting married again, possibly to someone from the church. It was very common for church members to marry each other back then, and I suppose it made sense because they would have things in common and would both know other folk in the church, so it would be 'safer' than just going out into the wide world to find a mate. Whatever, Dad was desperate to have his family back in one piece with a mother for his children. He was still only forty-one and wasn't ready to live the rest of his life without someone to share it with.

The funeral. The huge church seemed to be bursting at the seams with hundreds of people: they even had to put extra seats in at the back. All these people who loved Mum turned up to pay their respects – people she had worked with, people from the church, relatives, friends, neighbours... The local newspaper had carried around sixty tributes to Mum during that week, which was a shock in itself, seeing your own mum written about in so many words of friendship, admiration, affection and love, and all of those words saying that she was gone now, forever.

When they brought the coffin out of the funeral car, and I knew her poor cold body was inside that wooden box, I felt a massive jolt, as if someone really powerful had punched all the breath out of me. We held hands and walked behind the coffin, almost in slow motion as if we would never really get anywhere... or maybe I just wanted us to stay like that, frozen in time, with Mum still there with us somehow, not buried in the ground.

Everyone was singing. It was loud and lovely – emotional and full of energy. I had chosen one of the hymns and when they began singing the words I wanted Mum to hear, I saw her brother crying. Mum's only sibling, he was completely devastated. Finally, for the first time, I cried, too. But, even then, I fought hard to keep my feelings in check because of all those people who were watching us. I saw some of Mum's colleagues who had known her well, all weeping and sobbing. So much true expression of grief, of loss. The whole funeral was a mass of emotion.

At the graveside, we children were held back from seeing the coffin lowered down – once again, it was someone else who thought that would be for the best. As a distraction, I counted the flower tributes and wreaths, and I remember there were eighty-four altogether. After the burial, they were all placed on and around the grave, making a little mountain of colour and beauty. I know there was a reception afterwards, but I have no memory of it at all.

And so, life carried on. While Dad was at work, Grandma looked after us and we ate, slept, walked and talked like everyone else. All of those people at the funeral – we never saw any of them again, not one. Except family, of course. It was like nothing had happened, but it had, and our world would never be the same again.

Chapter 4: A New Start

Dad's talk of re-marrying was obviously more than the shock of losing Mum, because he started seeing a lady – and yes, she was a member of our church. Her name was Shirley and she'd known Mum for years, just like everyone knew everyone else in the congregation.

Shirley had never been married before and she didn't have any children, so it must have been a daunting prospect for her to consider taking on a readymade family – especially as Michael, Megan and I were not the most willing participants in the new arrangement.

It felt strange, being a bridesmaid at my dad's wedding with Mum gone only a little over a year. What made it more uncomfortable was that I was walking down the aisle of our church, Mum's church. And watching Dad marry someone else was not something I would ever have wanted to do.

I think what made our new life so much more difficult for us was that we'd been happy, truly content as a family until Mum was taken from us so tragically. Shirley must have thought we were spoiled, and I can sort of understand that because she was from a big family of thirteen children who had lived through the war years, so they couldn't have had an easy time of it.

Mealtimes soon turned into something of a problem for her because she saw us as ungrateful brats, but it was simply that we weren't used to saying 'thank you' for everything that was put in front of us, and Shirley served up minced beef way too often, which we all hated, so there was no way we were going to let her think we were grateful. It really annoyed her whenever we would announce that we were 'starving' when we just fancied a bite to eat.

"You kids have no idea what it's like to starve," she'd say with a scowling face, and it was clear that her childhood had been very different from ours, and whatever experiences she'd lived through had given her a hard edge, making her appear cold and hostile.

Something a bit more important than mealtime behaviour – Shirley had no money of her own, so right after they were married – in fact, it was the day after the wedding – Dad took her to his solicitor and changed his Will in her favour. She had insisted that he leave everything to her and we children would get nothing. That would never have been Dad's idea, but he was a softie and Shirley certainly wore the trousers. Grandma couldn't believe what he'd done. She was devastated.

We had to get used to this new way of life, but we weren't at all happy about it. Even though Shirley tried her best with us, things never really improved and it felt as if all of the joy had gone from our family; we had to mind our Ps and Qs and always be careful of how we spoke so that we didn't upset her. It wasn't easy, but my way of dealing with it was to be even more of a 'good girl' at home than I'd been before.

Exactly nine months into the marriage, baby Leo was born, our tiny half-brother. His arrival was the best thing that could have happened, as this brand new little person seemed to bring us all together in our shared focus on him. He was a lovely baby, always happy and smiling, and we were so thrilled to have him in our lives, we even brought our teacher home to see him!

Sadly, as much as Leo's sunny presence improved things for a while, we still struggled with being this new step-family and, as time passed, so the cracks deepened. Megan seemed to be constantly arguing and fighting with our step-mother, and poor Dad must have been tearing himself in two, trying not to fall out with his new wife and keeping his children happy at the same time. Shirley remained very cold towards us and never made us feel at all welcome.

Of course, we always had our bolt-hole just across the road at Grandma's and that's exactly where you'd find us when things got difficult. That can't have been good for our relationship with Shirley, racing off to tell tales every time something or other didn't suit us, but we were children and we felt safe with Grandma when sometimes life didn't feel safe at all.

After a while, Dad sold our house and we moved

away from what we knew, from everything that was familiar, and from dear, sweet Grandma, the only stability in our young lives. The new house never really felt like home.

As soon as she could, Megan found employment in a hotel on the south coast. Even better, because the hours were sometimes unsociable, a room in the staff quarters came with the job. She couldn't wait to get away. Unfortunately for her, and probably because she was still quite young and had never been away from home before, she became quite homesick and wanted to come back. I felt sorry for her, having to eat humble pie and ask Dad and Shirley to let her move back in, but Shirley had never been able to cope with Megan, given my sister's rather challenging behaviour, and so my poor sis was told that baby Leo had moved into her old room so there simply wasn't the space. Megan was taken in by the family of an old school friend who were very kind to her, so maybe it all worked out for the best – but now my 'family' was feeling more broken than ever.

Shirley doted on her little boy and he always had the best of everything, especially when it came to birthday and Christmas gifts. We were older now and didn't need the attention Leo required, so this situation served to make us feel even more rejected, alienated... it was difficult for everyone.

Leo was Shirley's only child, a tiny infant and totally dependent on his mother; we'd reached our teen years and this was something she had no idea how to cope with. Somehow, we carried on appearing 'normal' on the outside, especially when going to church, just as we'd done all of our lives.

I started college but wasn't really interested, and my lack of enthusiasm for further education didn't improve when I found my very first boyfriend, Steve. All we ever did was hold hands, but I thoroughly enjoyed visiting his house: his family were just that – a real *proper* family, not two different families trying to be one and failing miserably.

The inevitable happened when I reached seventeen. I left home. Megan had sorted herself out and was living down in Torquay where she had a job in a small family-run hotel with her own accommodation. I had made up my mind that I wanted to get into nursing but I had to wait until I was eighteen to begin training, so the plan was that I would stay with Megan for a year. I packed my things and set off into the big wide world to join her. Dad was sad to let me go but he didn't do or say anything to try to change my mind. He knew it was for the best.

My first impression of Torquay was that I must be dreaming! Firstly, I was collected from the bus station by Megan's employer in his sleek black limousine and he was a lovely chatty man who spent the journey singing Megan's praises, telling me what a good little worker she was and how everyone adored her. It was a hot sunny day and the sea sparkled as we drove along under the palm trees that waved gently in the summer breeze. This was paradise. And I had just begun my very own adventure. I tingled with excitement at the idea of having some control over my own life, and I felt liberated, free at last.

And, to top it off, I got a job with Megan's employers, working in their other hotel a little way along the sea front – with my own room! Megan and I worked together a lot of the time and we did shifts in both hotels so we were kept busy. They let us take the same days off so that we could spend time together and we'd cycle for miles along the coast. It wasn't long before I had a great suntan and I was really fit from all the exercise. Megan had made some friends and they welcomed me into the group; we had barbecues on the beach or took boat trips around the shoreline. That year was a truly happy time.

To begin with, we both felt we should go to church. After a lifetime of attending as a family, it was very much a part of us and it wasn't easy to just change that, so we joined the local Baptist congregation because they had a lot of youngsters of our age group. Pretty soon, we had our own little gang of fellow church-goers and we'd socialise together as well as meet for the services. It seemed that every one of us was at a crossroads in our lives and we were all a bit lost, so getting together was natural and we were comfortable with each other.

There was soon one person in that group who became special to me and I found myself falling in love for the first time.

Chapter 5: First Love, First Heartbreak

One girl, one boy. Both young, both vulnerable. Both with a lot to learn about life. He was tall and slim, fit, good-looking, and he had a decent job in a bank. He seemed so mature, so much older and wiser than his years. We were both just seventeen. But, at the time, it seemed it was our destiny to be together.

His name was Philip. Phil. Outwardly, he was friendly and sociable, well adjusted and appeared to be happy with his life. In reality, life as he had known it was being turned upside-down. An only child, he felt abandoned when both of his parents, in the middle of their divorce, began new relationships with people Phil didn't know, and both moved away from the area to be with their new partners. He was left to live on his own in the now empty house that had once been his family home. His relatives on both sides all lived in the Midlands, from where his parents had relocated years earlier. So, Phil was now alone, unhappy and desperate for something better.

Although we were both members of the young people's church group, we only really started to get to know each other at the gym. He was keen on sports and keeping fit, especially running. He would run for miles on his own. One of my friends told me, "Phil's just joined, he needs someone to show him the ropes."

He was so attractive, not just physically with his long legs, brown eyes with sweeping lashes and that gorgeous smile, but I could tell he was a good person on the inside, too. Charming, and with a lovely gentle sense of humour... I was smitten!

We chatted and soon we were telling each other things about our lives that normally weren't easy to say. But with him it was easy, and it seemed he felt the same. He told me how he had felt when his parents divorced, and he didn't even have a brother or sister to share the devastation. I told him how it had been for me when I suddenly lost my mum and then, before I'd really come to terms with her death, my dad had started seeing someone else.

We shared all of our history, our secrets, our hopes and dreams. We became an 'item' and it was wonderful. Before long, we were discussing marriage, and even having a family at some point. It was our first true love, for both of us. I was so happy.

Looking back, I guess having both lost our real families, we were driven to building our own, something solid, something to fill that aching void.

The hotels Megan and I had been working in, and

where we had rooms, were closed for the season so we had to find some digs. We rented a really small, but very cheap, basement flat. She and I both found other jobs so we could just afford the rent, the electricity, the gas, the laundry... but it was difficult. In winter the place was dreadful, unbelievably cold, and we'd go down the road to sit in the launderette for a while, just to get warm. Dad and his new wife didn't seem to care about us, about how we were struggling just to get by, and it was the same for Phil, with neither of his parents in their new lives appearing to even wonder how he was managing.

I had applied for nursing training and eventually I had an offer of a place – at King's College in London, about 200 miles away! We knew it wouldn't be easy but we gave our promise to each other to make the long-distance relationship work. It was a difficult three years, especially as I was surrounded by fellow students who all had their partners nearby, but Phil and I spoke on the phone as often as we could, and every month I'd take the train back to Torquay, to be with him for a brief, but wonderful, time.

Hurray! I qualified! And I had a post lined up in Newton Abbot, a short and easily managed journey from home. Phil was well on his way to promotion and our world was looking very exciting, indeed. We decided to get engaged.

Thanks to Phil's job at the bank, we were able to buy a house with a favourable mortgage, and the next stepping-stone was to get married. Our wedding was amazing – a tiny stone church in a picturesque village, the sun beaming down on our special day, and we even had our families there, all seemingly happy for us. All of our friends, work colleagues and neighbours helped us celebrate our love and commitment to each other. What a glorious day!

Our first year as man and wife passed by happily, but along the way I was noticing more and more of my friends were having babies, and I quickly became very keen to have a child of our own, as if that would complete our little family – possibly still an effect of the feelings of abandonment we had both experienced. We did try, but by the end of that year, I still wasn't pregnant.

Life continued to be kind to us. We moved to a bigger, better house, bought a little boat, we took regular holidays and drove a really nice car. But, everywhere I looked, I saw babies. Babies in prams, women carrying babies, little toddlers on wobbly legs, and – worst of all – ladies with bumps, happily pregnant. I felt even more desperate in my obsession to have the baby that eluded me.

Phil's career was progressing in leaps and bounds now, and he was invited to be part of a management group of his peers who were being sent on one of those personal development projects that meant being away from home for two weeks and doing things like lighting a fire on a cold, dark hillside in the middle of the night without matches or a lighter. I've always wondered how that can possibly help anyone to be a good manager, but I'm told it's all about character building and teamwork. I just know I wouldn't fancy it!

I didn't get a call, or even a text, over those two weeks but I assumed it was part of the course to be cut off from civilisation, so I didn't worry about it. It did feel a bit odd, though.

The wanderer returned and I couldn't wait to hug him, to feel his arms around me, to be 'us' again. But I noticed a difference in Phil straight away. Something else I noticed was that he had acquired a really good suntan. He was somehow distant, sort of not really there, not the same – one of those things you can't put your finger on. From the moment he was back, work took over and he was hardly ever at home, spending all of his time either at the office or out with his colleagues. I tried to understand. The course had obviously changed everything, changed him. I wondered if I was supposed to be happy about this, happy that he had now obviously really taken to the life of a more senior manager, both from the work point of view and socially, too. That was how it had to be for him to succeed, didn't it? Our relationship had dropped into second place and we weren't even having sex any more. That really hurt.

Less than a month after he came home, we had just sat down to dinner when Phil looked at me with an expression I'd never seen before, never wanted to see on the face of the man I loved.

"I'm so sorry, Paula... I really don't want us to have a baby." He paused, and I thought I saw a flicker of pain in his eyes for a fleeting moment. "And I don't want to be married any longer... so sorry."

Although it would be easy for anyone looking in from the outside to say the writing was on the wall, when it's you it happens to, you never see it coming. His words hit me like a speeding train, threw me into a whirlwind of shock and dismay. We sat there, not speaking, and I wept uncontrollably. What was happening? I was hurt, angry, devastated. I felt cheated, deceived in the worst way. How could he be denying me our baby now, after all we'd done, all we'd built together? I suddenly started throwing questions at him. How could he say that? What had I done wrong? And so on. But Phil had no answers for me.

He got up from the table and went upstairs, packed a bag and left. He said very quietly as he walked out of the front door, "I'll be staying at Mum's for a while."

But he didn't go to his mum's.

I spent the most miserable two weeks with him gone, tearing myself apart over what had happened, trying to find answers. But none came. After that, and it felt like months, Phil turned up at the house and my heart jumped – he'd come back! It was all going to be fine again... then I noticed he wasn't wearing his wedding ring and the truth of this awful situation dawned on me in a split second. He'd been with someone else. I'd lost him to another woman. The mystery suntan he'd come home with was from the beach he'd been lying on with her, and I realised everyone he worked with would have known all along. I was the last one to find out.

I followed him around the house, tears streaming, as he packed everything he owned, and with every little item that went into the bags and boxes, a piece of my heart went with them. And then he was gone.

I was humiliated, betrayed, defeated. Looking back, we were too young, too damaged by what we'd both been through, and we were doomed to fail. Eventually, I picked up the pieces. The divorce proceedings began, the house was sold and there I was, alone, unwanted, just like before.

Chapter 6: Meeting John

Divorce – especially when it's the other person's decision – is incredibly cruel. I couldn't get my head around how Phil had gone off with someone else, had an affair behind my back, destroyed the life we'd been building together, and rode off into the sunset to live happily ever after with my replacement. Whereas I was the one left behind, lonely and heartbroken, not understanding what had happened or why, the one who had to pack up and go back home, admitting to the disaster that had befallen my fairytale marriage.

The idea of staying in Torquay was too painful and I just wanted to get away. By this time, my relationship with Dad was not at all as I wanted it to be; now that he was with Shirley, there didn't seem to be any room for me in his life. But at least they gave me somewhere to stay and to store my worldly goods. I was grateful to be with family; I suppose it felt safe.

But how I wished my mother could be there, to listen, to understand, to say all the right things and to comfort me. I think that's when the harsh reality of her death truly hit home. I needed her now, more than ever. No Mum, no husband, and no baby. I was lost, adrift on a vast ocean of loneliness and pain. I couldn't really open up to Dad and Shirley, not about how I was feeling, and the heaps of my belongings, once lovingly arranged around the place Phil and I had called home, seemed to sneer down at me, an unwelcome reminder of what a failure I was. I didn't fit in anywhere – not at home, not with my career, because having to move had meant all I could find for work were poorly paid and irregular temp jobs, and I didn't feel I belonged in Bedfordshire. I just didn't belong. Full stop.

Time passed by... I was trying to get a permanent placement in one of the local hospitals and I'd found some decent private work through a professional agency; I'd managed to buy myself a little run-about car, and actually started to make new friends. But all of this was purely superficial, and underneath I was struggling. I still loved Phil, even though he'd hurt me so badly, I missed him and I missed the life we'd shared. No-one else could hold a candle to my memories of him, the feelings I carried were so strong, so real.

And yet, somewhere deep inside, I knew that I'd made the right move to go back home, to begin whatever my new life was going to be. Once the darkly depressing months of winter had dragged by, I made a decision to look for a little place to buy, somewhere I could call my own. A new home in a quiet village – that would be lovely. And the 1980s property market had provided me with the financial advantage of selling at a good price in the South to buy for much less further north.

The cash I got from the sale of the marital home in Torquay was far in excess of what I needed to buy my place in the sticks. My career had fallen into place and that led to being able to get a mortgage, with my new permanent post in a modern hospital of excellent reputation and a nursing team who shared an enlightened attitude and an immoveable dedication to the work.

So, it would seem that I was 'moving on' and things were looking up for me. I did see the positive in my new situation, yet I couldn't shake off my depression. I suppose we all have a basic survival instinct – whatever it was, I knew I had to conquer my feelings and get myself out of this miserable frame of mind.

Step One: A Night Out. By nature, I'd always been quiet and rather shy, never the party animal, but something in me was planning a rebellion of its own. I called my brother's girlfriend, Carol, and asked her if she fancied a girls' night out in town. She said yes. We started with a couple of drinks (in my case, probably mainly for Dutch courage) then headed into the town centre to the nightclub on St Peter's Street. Sweetings – the 'in' place to be. Great dance music, a buzzing atmosphere and the best light show in the area. We danced the night away, had a drink at the bar and I actually felt quite relaxed, and even managed to smile. A breakthrough, indeed!

The downside to being in a crowded place full of strangers was that, every now and then, I'd catch a glimpse of someone and my heart would start pounding – could it be him? Is that Phil? Then I'd realise, of course, that it wasn't him and the gloom would wash over me again. It was a real test and I felt like bursting into tears there on the dance floor, but I kept going, kept dancing, smiling...

Being with Carol was good for me because she was happy and settled in her relationship with Michael and so was definitely *not* available for anything more than a quick chat with any of the various lads whose attention we had obviously attracted. This kept me from doing anything silly – not that I was even tempted because none of these young men were Phil and I was nowhere close to being over him. And the divorce wasn't finalised yet, so I was still technically married. That evening wasn't about finding a new romance, it was just the first stage of getting out and about, socialising, surrounding myself with other people's enjoyment in the hope that eventually it would rub off.

Later in the evening, something happened. At first, it was something and nothing. Two rather worse-for-wear young chaps pushed their way through the crowd towards us and one of them was a bit persistent in his attempts to get my attention, so we moved away. They followed. The overly persistent one asked me what I wanted to drink, so, rather than offend him, I told him I was drinking Malibu and pineapple.

He kept forgetting what I'd said and had to ask me three or four times, but eventually the drink arrived and we chatted for a while – if you can call shouting over very loud music chatting! His pal had ambled off somewhere and he just stood there between the two of us until I signalled to him that we were going back on the dance floor.

He asked for my phone number. I was a bit shocked, but as I was also a bit tipsy, I scribbled the number on a scrap of paper and handed it to him as we manoeuvred our way back into the bopping crowd.

I didn't really remember much about him, except that he was tall and dark, and quite smartly dressed in a very colourful shirt and trendy narrow tie. His name was John.

The following week was full, with work and getting ready to move into my new house – my own home! One day, I arrived back at Dad's place to be told someone had been trying to reach me on the phone, someone called John, and would I call him back? NO! What a cheek! I'd never imagined for one second that he would actually call me. A few days later, another call from John and, again, I wasn't at home when he rang. My hours at the hospital varied so I wasn't the easiest person to catch at home.

He was not going to give up easily, that was clear. John rang time and time again, and after a while the law of averages kicked in and I was actually at home when he phoned. He asked me if I would go on a date with him and I have to say I found him rather charming, altogether different from the drunken stranger at the nightclub. He was very complimentary and I was flattered. He seemed to be a bit smitten with me!

....

We agreed to meet at a bar in town one evening. As it turned out, I had to stay late at work and had no way of contacting him so I stood him up and felt a bit guilty, but decided that surely he would give up the chase now. No! Once again, we made a date but he was taking no chances this time and said he'd meet me out of work then we could go to the bar together. He really did seem very keen.

And so we met, and I realised I had no real memory of his physical looks from that first night, and he was totally the opposite of the guy who had, apparently, gained his confidence by drinking quite a lot. Now sober, he was sort of geeky-looking with his dark-rimmed specs and scruffy clothes, and I noticed straight away an oddness about him, as if he wasn't comfortable with himself. He certainly wasn't someone who took an interest in how others saw him – something I did find rather strange, considering how persistent he'd been in trying to get me to meet him. He was obviously uneasy and wasn't very good at eye contact, which made him seem rather distant and self-absorbed.

Instead of putting me off, his boyish naivete appealed to me and I felt some empathy for him. I told myself I'd give him a chance, and that decision was in no small way based on his knowledge of, and interest in, sailing.

Having lived in Torquay, I was used to boats being a big part of everyday life, and it's one of the things I was missing a lot. And being so far from the coast now, it wasn't easy to find people who were involved in sailing, so I was quite pleased to have met someone who sailed, and I thought how lovely it would be to meet his boating friends as well, and finally get to know some like-minded folk and expand my social circle.

John told me his family were in luggage manufacturing, doing very well for the past few years after starting from humble beginnings with stalls on various markets. I kept thinking maybe he was just spinning me a line and his real job was probably packing boxes in some factory. It's not that I'm suspicious of people, it's more that there was something really odd about him that I couldn't explain, something that made me doubt him. It didn't help that he seemed to be shy when it came to making eye contact with me – I think most people would find that off-putting.

I knew he wasn't 'my type' but he did have a sort of 'little boy lost' appeal, and I was lonely and very keen to make new friends who I would have things in common with, so I pushed aside my doubts and just carried on seeing him, but I did make it clear we were friends, and nothing more. Looking back now, how I wish I had listened to my intuition.

The family business was indeed as John had

described, and he was totally driven by his work and his place in the company, completely engrossed in it every minute of every day. It was his life. I'd never known anyone with such energy, not just for work but for going places, having adventures, doing things. He was always on the go, never one for sitting still. And I was impressed with his appetite for life, for everything. His knowledge of sailing was vast and his enthusiasm greater, but even when we were chatting about this shared passion, I still didn't feel entirely easy with John.

Whenever he became deep in thought – which was quite a lot of the time – his face would become contorted, all screwed up, and he would stroke the bridge of his nose constantly for several minutes. My early assessment of him as being shy soon changed when I started getting to know him: he was elusive, distant and vague. Whenever I asked him something, I would be answered with a short, almost curt, reply that never went beyond minimal information, exactly the response to my question but nothing more than that. I felt for him, he was so inept when it came to human relationships, and I believed I could get him to open up to me. Something of a challenge, but I honestly wanted to help my strange new friend.

It became clear quite early on that John's life revolved around business because this was an area where he excelled. Normally appearing shy and withdrawn, when it came to winning over clients or suppliers, he was in a league of his own: he was charming, eloquent and in control. No matter who he was dealing with, no matter how high up the food chain they were, he would get his own way by being cool and confident. Not at all the odd individual I was getting to know, nothing like. This was so intriguing...

Once I was having a problem with someone at work and when I told John about it he advised me to square up to this person and use foul language to tell them how I felt! Of course, I never did, but I wondered why John seemed to have such little respect for other people, and yet he wanted to be respected by everyone. I found all of his quirks oddly endearing and, anyway, I felt safe because this was just friendship, nothing more. No way would I ever be involved fully with someone like him.

And yet, he was charming. And then he began to – in old-fashioned terms – woo me. It could have been that he realised he wasn't getting anywhere with me, but whatever it was, I was having a wonderful new life laid at my feet. And I liked it.

I can't remember how many gastro pubs and village eateries we visited, but they were all amazing and money was no object. I did offer to pay my share but John liked to spend his cash. We would sit in the gardens of white-washed cottage restaurants by mossy stone walls adorned with climbing roses, breathing the heady perfume of honeysuckle on a summer's evening, the rough-hewn wooden furniture and pristine table setting creating the perfect picture of fine dining, and John would always tell me to order anything I fancied. The wine lists were always impressive and the food would have satisfied the ancient gods. And still, John would turn up wearing his mis-matched outfits topped off with some old hooded zip-up jacket – in case the weather changed.

He took me to Scotland for Hogmanay once. We stayed in a charming little B&B with all the trimmings, including a big welcoming log fire and hot chocolate made with a generous measure of single malt whisky. When it came to the New Year celebrations, which the Scots are so famous for, we were having a great time until the midnight countdown began and suddenly, without a word, John was gone! I stood there, surrounded by hugging couples, kissing couples, and there I was – on my own. When he returned just after midnight, I asked him where he'd been and said the loo. How odd!

Something I found surprising was that he was brilliant at buying the right gifts for me, which he did a lot. He'd obviously notice when I admired something, a bracelet or a scarf or whatever in the shops, and he would surprise me with it later. He would pretend to buy a birthday present for a female relative and I'd be asked to help him choose – later that day, it would be mine. I have to say, this kind of thing can turn a girl's head! I was flattered, pleased, impressed – John was finally having an effect on me. I realised the hurt Phil had left me with was fading at last, a bit more each day, and I knew that was because of John.

Before long, I started to have deeper feelings for him than just friendship. He was certainly odd, weird even, but he was exciting, impulsive, and he obviously cared for me. I was in a good place now. My career was going well, I was earning a decent salary, I had my lovely little house and my car... I was healing.

One of John's female pals said something to me that made a big difference. She had worked out that our friendship might be moving forward and she told me, "I know he's a bit strange, bless him, but he'll never hurt you."

That was all I needed to hear. We started dating officially. John's persistence had paid off.

Never hurt me. Oh, the irony.

Chapter 7: Discord and Doubts...

The relationship continued. John was constantly surprising me with little outings, weekend trips away and well chosen gifts, all of which delighted me, of course. We visited the loveliest far-off places where we were 'away from it all', surrounded by stunning natural countryside or in a remote seaside location where the only crowds were the seagulls picking among the rocks for their dinner. We'd stroll in peaceful woodlands, by trickling streams, along shell-strewn sandy beaches, and then there would be dinner at another gorgeous little bistro.

I was impressed at his ability to always choose things that I couldn't help but be happy with, and all of which worked on my feelings for him in a very positive way. I saw him as making an effort to make me happy. It was perfect. Almost.

Something I always wondered about, and I never found out why John had a problem with this, was his total lack of interest in my former existence, the early years with my family, Maybe because I'd lost my mother, I felt a need to share that part of me with my partner, to tell him about my parents, my brother and sister, and how happy life had been as a child. I had my photo albums, crammed with images of our days out, picnics, having fun, Christmas festivities and such like; a box full of cine films that Mum and Dad had taken over the years, of birthdays, family get-togethers with lots of laughter and sharing. So many lovely memories, and an ideal way for John to get to know me better, to learn about who I was, where I came from.

But, no matter how I tried to talk to him about my past, he wouldn't listen, wouldn't ask any questions – nothing, not the slightest interest. He really didn't want to know, and this upset me deeply because my background was important to me and I wanted him to know everything about me. But John was immoveable, and I could do nothing to change that.

I did find that aspect of our relationship most frustrating, but we are all individuals, all very different people, and no-one should expect another person to have the same wants and needs as they have – isn't that right? When you form a bond with someone you accept them for whatever they are, warts and all, don't you? Never try to change someone: I knew that would be wrong, so I kept reminding myself of all the good things, the things that felt right about being with John. And I carried on.

We did, however, talk about *his* past, his memories of family life as a youngster. He'd had the most 'wonderful childhood', the best of everything, and he'd never had to go without. He described it as a 'proper' childhood and obviously believed no-one else could come close – or maybe no-one else could *compete*?

There was one memory that had stayed with him, of being in hospital for quite a while when he was only a toddler, and in those days there was no way parents could stay overnight with their child, so he had cried and screamed for his parents all the time he was there. To me, this seemed a normal thing for such a young child to do, being separated from family for the first time, but I wondered why he had needed to tell me.

We reached that time in our relationship when I was to meet his mother. I'd already met his dad through their work and he was a most likeable character, but when it came to meeting his mum I did feel rather anxious. I'd heard so much about her – an awesome description of a strong-willed, defiant woman who was used to getting her own way, or else! She suffered from schizophrenia and was permanently on strong medication. A bit daunting, to say the least. But I told myself, *Come on, girl, you're a trained nurse with some mental health experience and your own mother suffered with depression and was always at the mercy of her nerves and the medications she had to take...*

With this in mind, I convinced myself that I was ready to meet My Boyfriend's Mother. I decided to take a really good box of chocolates for her.

Their house was quite large, detached with a good-sized front garden, on the edge of a picturesque village where you could imagine everyone knew everyone else and they were all friendly and chatty. John opened the door and I noticed straight away the many old pictures hanging on the walls, and any spaces between them were taken up by smaller cameo-type frames displaying those ancient sepia photos of non-smiling people who looked as though they were being photographed at gunpoint.

There were also lots of old-fashioned ornaments from years gone by, huge vases standing on the worn carpet, smaller items crowding together atop the shelves of an ornately carved dark wooden hall stand. Long strands of cobweb hung from the tarnished, but still elaborate, light fitting. At the same instant, I noticed the unmistakeable aroma of dogs that were never groomed, and there was pet hair clinging to the almost threadbare chair upholstery and cushions. Some people would have been put off, I know, but in my 'glass half full' opinion, my first thought was *Thank heaven! She's no domestic goddess and she'll probably never even consider judging me for my housework standards.* There I go again – judgement, and from someone I've not even met.

As the door to the lounge opened, I caught sight of her, sitting in a big wingback chair with tapestry cushions, the colours a mere shadow of their undoubted original brilliance. In front of her and within reach, an ornate glass ashtray the size of a soup bowl, almost full of cold grey ash and cigarette tips, each with its own smear of red lipstick. Beside the ashtray stood a crystal cut glass tumbler, half full of amber liquid that I later realised was whisky. One hand rested in her lap and the other was held in mid-air, fingers gripping another cigarette, newly lit even though a thin wisp of smoke was still rising from the heap of ash. The walls and paintwork were stained with nicotine, and smoke filled the room, pervading everything in its reach.

It was disgusting, offensive. But I stood my ground, trying to make my breathing as shallow as I could and wondering if I would need my inhaler at some point. Since a chest infection when I was young, I'd been prescribed one as a 'just in case' measure and hardly ever needed to use it, but this place was a challenge for any breathing being.

I stood quite still, smiling at this woman who appeared to be ignoring me, as if to make a point. Tilting her head back slightly, she closed her eyes and drew deeply on the cigarette as if her life depended on it, and then exhaled very slowly, emitting a cloud of smoke and appearing to be lost in the experience.

She was a large woman, her face a portrait of bitterness and scorn, qualities no doubt well practised over the years. It was hard to believe she had only just turned fifty. Her large dark glasses did nothing to enhance her looks, and every time she put the cigarette to her lips and moved her head back a little, a lock of unkempt brown hair fell against her neck, touching the ragged edge of the tatty old blue fleece hanging round her shoulders. Every now and then, she'd lift the tumbler and take a gulp of whisky. I felt I'd been standing there for hours. I admit it, she scared the pants off me.

Everything in this room was old, faded memorabilia from past lives in the form of ornaments and framed pictures, rugs and cushions, china and trinkets, like a weird competition to see if every square inch of every surface could be covered, obliterated with something, rather than nothing.

She was studying me now, and I was convinced she wasn't going to make any effort to get on with me, or even to get to know me. When I heard John call her Sandra instead of 'Mum', it seemed strange and made me rather uncomfortable. At last, she spoke, but only to ask me questions now and then, and I could hear the nervous shake in my voice as I replied. Then, turning her head away, she added, "I don't like chocolates, by the way."

John and I went into the kitchen to make some tea. Another very old-fashioned room where even more ornaments and bric-a-brac adorned every bit of space. Dirty pots were piled up in the sink! If this had been a home visit to a patient in my professional life, I would have been very concerned about this lady's situation. But John was behaving as if nothing was amiss, as if all of this decaying chaos was perfectly normal, so I made the effort and just tried to avoid the areas most heavily polluted by cigarette smoke. After half an hour or so, I said I thought it was time for us to go.

It had been a difficult experience for me in many ways, but John insisted that his mother was fine "once you get to know her" and he made light of the whole mad afternoon. I knew they had a strong relationship and he wouldn't hear anything said in criticism of her, so I put the strange episode behind me.

Meanwhile, John had met my dad and Shirley at their house. Although I never mentioned it, I found great personal amusement in Dad's front room having a shelf on which there stood a Bible text plaque that read "God is our refuge and strength, a very present help in trouble. Psalm 46:1", while at John's family home the equivalent shelf displayed boxes of cigarettes and several empty cut glass tumblers! I enjoyed the irony and was confident that John and I would laugh about the obvious extreme differences in our childhood lives. Finding shared humour in it would unite us; after all, love overcomes everything, doesn't it?

But was this love? The poem-writing, stay-at-home 'me' who Phil had left sad and alone had been determined I would never love again, had believed that 'first love is the deepest' and all of the other romantic notions we humans adopt when nursing a broken heart and a dented ego.

Months passed by and we carried on dating, being a couple, but I never did feel that pulse-racing, heart-pounding anticipation when I was meeting John, no butterflies in the tummy, no tingle when we accidentally touched hands over the dinner table. It was more that we had settled into the routine of the relationship and I assumed this was how it should be now.

One morning I awoke to a terrible wave of nausea

and felt strange, badly out of sorts. As I blinked the sleep from my eyes, the realisation hit me! Pregnant? Surely not! All the time I'd been with Phil, I'd wanted a baby desperately but we'd never managed it, so how could I be pregnant now, when John and I had been using contraception? This couldn't be right.

I had actually reached a point where I accepted that infertility was my fate, and that could have made me a little lax with the precautions at times. I was so sure it wasn't necessary. Before I could mention anything to John, I needed to find out for certain, so I bought a test kit and – there it was in the double blue line – I was really pregnant!

Immediately, the tears came. Tears of – what? Shame? Yes, I was a divorced woman in a relationship of only a few months with a man I hardly knew. What would people say? People at church? I started to feel judged and yet I hadn't told one single person. Tears of confusion? Yes, why now? Just when I'd got my new life sorted – good job, my own home, the mortgage that took most of my salary... And what about John? Would he be happy with this, or would he drop me like a hot potato? And tears of relief? Relief at discovering I *can* have a baby, I *can* be a mum. Relief that I can make my own family at last?

I saw John the next evening at my place. As usual, he was talking business and I almost had to hold my hand up like a kid at school so I could speak. "John, there's something I have to tell you..." I was shaking. "I'm pregnant."

His face turned pale and his eyes flashed angrily. "You can't be! You can't have children..."

"I know, that's what I believed for ages, but I've taken a test and it's positive."

"No! This can't be happening! I hope you're joking..."

"I'm not joking. I'm pregnant and you're going to be a dad."

His wine glass hit the coffee table and shattered. He was *not* happy. "You lied to me, you bitch! I don't want a fucking baby! Get rid of it! How selfish are you? What will my mother say? A baby? With a divorced woman I've only just met? She'd be appalled!"

Somewhere in among his tirade of insults and rejection, I started to cry. For years, this was everything I wanted, but my timing couldn't have been worse.

"If you keep it, I'm off! Don't expect any help from me – you're on your own!" The door slammed shut. John was gone.

I needed to think, and I couldn't face going to work so I took a few days off, which was just as well because the morning sickness got worse, and it was no respecter of time of day. I was throwing up morning, noon and night. John stayed away, not even a phone call to see how I was. I felt alone, frightened, and I couldn't bring myself to turn to my family. I had no idea what I was going to do.

Days passed, and then John appeared, all sweetness and light – the John I liked. He said he'd come up with a plan. His 'plan', which he dressed up in terms of "thinking logically", "jetting off somewhere romantic in the sun" and "putting all of this behind us", roughly translated to him telling me we could stay together and have babies in the future, we could get married properly – a nice big wedding – and he would support me and our children. And so on, and so on – "but not like this".

I didn't say anything and he continued, more forcefully this time, but still calm and controlled. He threatened to drive over to my dad's and tell him and Shirley. "Imagine your dad's shame! His daughter, divorced and now pregnant – and no father for the baby in sight."

I was sobbing but he showed no compassion. "Shut up! Let's go now and tell him, come on, get in the car. If you won't tell him, I will."

I actually got in the car, still sobbing my heart out, and feeling sick and hopeless. He drove and we headed for my dad's house. As we pulled up outside, I knew I couldn't do it. I couldn't put my dad through this.

"Take me home, John, please?"

"OK, but you have to promise you'll get rid of it and we never mention this again."

This was my last chance saloon, or that's how it felt.

"OK."

John made the arrangements and paid the fee at the clinic. I couldn't come to terms with what I was about to do: it was as if I'd been drugged or hypnotised. I was certain God would never forgive me. The first commandment is "Thou shalt not kill" and now I was a murderer, but I could never tell anyone. God would know and He would judge me... I would go to hell.

John took me to the clinic and said he'd pick me up at seven o'clock that evening. I was in a sort of trance, however pathetic that sounds, my head was a whirl of questions, doubts, fears... and then it was all over. Consumed with guilt and self-hatred, I tried to think of the shame and shock I had spared my family, the upset I had avoided for everyone. That didn't really help.

We drove home in silence. I was thinking to myself, I really should end this relationship. I would get my strength back and I would tell him soon, once I felt better and my head wasn't so jumbled. As we drove along the streets, festive lights were all twinkling on the trees and people were out and about, doing their Christmas shopping. It wasn't lost on me, the irony of it being Christmas time – a new child born. Everyone was celebrating and enjoying this special time, but for me it was all dark depression and so much guilt. I made it through somehow, keeping up the pretence with my happy party face on. But I couldn't look any of my family in the eye, knowing what I had done. I'd even had to lie to work about my time off. It seemed I had become a different person, doing these things I never would have dreamed of doing before now, but once you start on that path of lies, covering up, deceit... you have to keep going. There's no turning back.

I was resolved to end things with John, but before

I did, there he was, walking through my door with a holiday brochure in his hand. He was excited, like a kid with a new toy, the John I really liked and enjoyed being with.

"Let's go to the Maldives! We can stay in a four-star hotel right by the beach!"

He booked the holiday and a few weeks later, off we went. We never spoke of the abortion again. While we were away, he seemed to be making an extra effort to please me, to entertain me and keep me busy. He wasn't one for lounging around a pool all day, so we swam, took boat trips, tried paragliding and walked for hours up in the hills, then had romantic dinners by candlelight. It was all good, all back to normal. As long as we didn't have to talk about anything deep and meaningful, about feelings.

We carried on the same for the next couple of years and everything was fine on the surface, but I couldn't forget our baby, couldn't let go of the guilt.

Passing a jeweller's shop one day, I glanced in the window and a rather beautiful ring caught my eye. I mentioned it, not for any reason other than I thought it was a lovely piece of jewellery. John dashed inside the shop and in seconds I was trying on that same ring. Forever the businessman, he bartered with the shop owner because he was paying in cash. How embarrassing! No proposal, just a quick Del Boy impression and then we were engaged. It didn't feel at all special.

The engagement raised a few eyebrows among

John's family. They couldn't imagine him married, settled down, no longer being a 'law unto himself' and it made me feel pretty proud that I was the one who got him to break that 'confirmed bachelor' mould.

I know every relationship has ups and downs and nothing is perfect, but during the months of our engagement I did see a side of John that I really should have taken as a warning, but I was so far down the road with him, I just couldn't see myself giving up on us, and so I turned a blind eye.

I did again when he slammed down on the accelerator as we were driving along a country lane on holiday and then stood on the brake, bringing the car to a sudden and juddering emergency stop – and made me get out and walk the mile back to the hotel. All because I had started singing along to something that was playing on the radio. And I did that time he became furious with the lawn mower when it wouldn't start, when he shoved me out of the way so hard I fell over and hurt my leg quite badly. He ignored me as I lay in a heap and carried on shouting and swearing at the poor lawn mower.

Maybe a part of my reluctance to do anything about the bad stuff was that I'd been gathering all of this baggage since I met John and I couldn't allow myself to believe that any decent man would want me after that. How sad is that?

Chapter 8: All Washed Up…

Although the bad times eventually became the norm, we did have good times and one of the most fun things we used to do was to take John's speedboat out on the sea. It was a smart little thing, with a very powerful engine that could really get up some speed, and I have to say, I was impressed. I loved our little trips out, when we'd skip over the waves in the sunshine and explore whatever coastline we had chosen to visit, stopping for lunch and then speeding back to our hotel.

We were in Cornwall one summer and decided to take the boat out so we could have a look around the nearby shore where there were little sheltered coves and tiny unspoilt beaches to enjoy. Lifejackets on, lunch packed and bottles of water in the cool box, with John at the wheel in his fun mood, we left the harbour and soon the little boat was skimming across the sparkling water and cutting through the waves. I found it exhilarating and would giggle with delight whenever the boat actually jumped out of the water!

We'd been out for a while and had stopped to eat, just bobbing about gently on the calm sea, a mile or so from land, when John suddenly became agitated and was impatient to get back. I had no idea what had brought on this change of mood, but then I never did. His face set in a scowl, he throttled the boat at full speed towards the harbour, which was a speck on the shoreline.

Then – BANG! What the hell? In an instant, the boat stopped dead as if it had run into a brick wall, hurtling the pair of us into the water, along with everything that wasn't fastened down. Disbelief. Shock. There we were, gulping seawater, the broken boat now sinking, our belongings floating around us, and the harbour seemed so very far away. Quiet.

The only sound was the cry of the seagulls as they swooped and dived to pick at the remains of our lunch. I think my nursing training must have kicked in at some point, and I tried to focus, to shake off the shock and work out what to do. I started to swim, hampered by the lifejacket but I knew I had to keep it on, then there came a surge of relief as I realised the tide was on its way in. John didn't speak at all. Anyway, we both needed all of our strength to make it to shore.

After what must have been half an hour, maybe more, we washed up in a little cove. The harbour was nowhere to be seen, but I was grateful just to be on land again. While I struggled from the surf on to the wet shingle, John lay there, not making any effort to get up, shaking his head and shouting, "See what you've done now!" His unbelievable attitude shocked me almost as much as the accident itself – how on earth could I be to blame for what had happened? We didn't even know what had caused it.

I checked to see if he was injured but, apart from a badly bruised ego, he was fine. He still made no attempt to do anything, and I could see the tide coming in quite quickly; it was only a matter of time before this cove would be under water. Then we'd be cut off and washed back out to sea. I had to think, and act fast. I looked all around, trying to work out my best plan of action. Behind me was the incoming sea, rolling ever closer, and in front of me was a craggy rock face. Bad choice, but the only thing I could do was try to climb up to the cliff top. I was no mountaineer, but there was a distinct lack of options: it was either climb or, quite possibly, end my life here.

I started, very gingerly, to grab hold of any jutting bits of rock above me and pull myself up, being careful where I put my feet before letting go of anything. After the forced long-distance swim, it was incredibly hard work and exhausting, not to mention terrifying, and still not a movement or a word of encouragement from John as I hauled myself up a bit at a time. I could hear him moaning on about his precious boat, of course, and blaming me for everything.

After goodness knows how long, and with absolutely no idea how I had done it, I made it to the top, breathless and sweating, bleeding gashes on my hands and arms, legs and knees, but that didn't matter. I had to get help. I could hear myself sobbing but I felt removed from everything – except my heartbeat, pounding, deafening.

Barely able to stand and gasping for breath, I gazed in every direction from that cliff top, mostly across wild meadowland stretching away as far as I could see. Then I saw it. A little house, some way off, the only sign of civilisation. Half stumbling, half walking, I pushed myself towards the place, praying that someone would be home. Then I heard a dog barking.

I must have looked such a sight, leaning on the wall of this lady's house, battered and bloody, my chest heaving, crying my eyes out and babbling wildly, waving one arm behind me in the general direction of the cove. Thankfully, this was the home of a lovely, kind lady who took me in without a second thought, all the while doing her best to comfort me and telling me everything would be fine, that the worst was over. She made me some hot, sweet tea, at the same time calling the coastguard on her phone. They arranged for John to be picked up immediately in a rescue dinghy, and they collected me and drove me back to the hotel.

I will never forget the kindness that lady showed me at a moment in my life when I was so desperately in need of help. It could so easily have been someone else, someone who would have shut the door in my face.

John never thanked me for what I did that day, never expressed one word of gratitude – in fact, we never even spoke of it after that. It was all about him and his boat.

Chapter 9: Getting Ready for the Big Day

Our wedding day was fast approaching. Looking back, I'm amazed we actually got to that point, but we did.

John and I had agreed all along that we should keep my divorce under wraps, especially when it came to his family. As my dad had convinced me to revert to my maiden name as quickly as possible, and we lived a long way from where I'd had that previous life with Phil, this wasn't difficult. But it did rear its head when we asked the local vicar to marry us in the C of E village church.

In those days, people married either in church or at a Register Office: there were no options to perform your ceremony up a mountain, under a tropical waterfall or while deep-sea diving, as can be organised today, and my divorce was causing our first stumbling block when we were told we couldn't possibly be married in church. However, as with most things in life, it's not *what* you know but *who* you know, and when I spoke to the vicar and explained that my entire family had always been regular church-goers, it turned out that he knew some of my relatives! He agreed to approach the bishop and ask for special permission. Luckily, the word came back that the church would comply with our request.

I was so utterly thankful, because I still believed that marriage and having a family was all about God, and, after everything that had happened, I really needed His blessing. I couldn't even consider a Register Office wedding – it had to be a *proper* wedding, nothing else would do. With the good news from the vicar, I felt redeemed, as though I was being given a second chance. John, on the other hand, wasn't at all bothered, except to be relieved that he could keep up the façade of me being his virgin bride, plus the church aspect was obviously important to his mother, because she wanted her precious son to have only the very best, the full Monty, frills and all.

Then there was the awkward situation between the two families, who didn't know each other, and who were worlds apart. John's parents had met Dad and Shirley when we all went out for dinner together, which I have to say was one of the most uncomfortable evenings of my entire life. Smoking in restaurants was not an issue in those days, and John's mother proceeded to light and puff on one cigarette after another, while knocking back a frightening volume of whisky and barely speaking a word to anyone.

John's dad, being the lovely man he was, and understanding that my dad's financial situation was nowhere close to his own, had very kindly settled the bill before my dad had a chance to offer to pay, which he had fully intended to do. John never let me forget that, telling me my dad should have made more effort to get his money out sooner. "Mean bastard!"

So, there I was, covering up a first marriage and divorce, covering up an abortion, feeling alienated from my family by the loss of my mother and my dad's re-marriage, desperate for a baby of my own, surrounded by two families who appeared to come from different planets, and – stupidly, I know – ignoring the question marks that kept appearing over my relationship with John. The perfect recipe for a successful marriage?

Just a few weeks before the Great Day, we found ourselves under pressure from family on both sides...

My sister, Megan, was happily married and had just given birth to her second son, but during the pregnancy she had suffered with depression. She and her new baby were admitted to a specialist unit in the hospital where I was working, so I was able to look in on them every day. Baby Karl was beautiful, but poor Megan was very ill and so the nurses were doing everything for him. Megan's husband, who loved her dearly, was busy working as hard as he could to pay the mortgage and bills. It was a sad and desperate situation.

After much family discussion, it was agreed that both of Megan's little boys should stay with Dad and

Shirley until things looked more positive for Megan and her husband. Shirley loved children and hadn't been able to have a brother or sister for little Leo, so she was only too happy to take the boys in.

In John's family, his sister, Celia, had just been abandoned by her husband when he disappeared over the horizon with their nanny. Celia was left literally holding the babies, her two very young children, and with no money, as hubby had frittered it all away. She was now at the mercy of John's family. Sandra immediately came to her daughter's rescue, no doubt pleased to have her back in the fold. She bought a house for Celia and the children, and a decent car for her to get around in.

So, although it was wonderful that both sides were helping out with their respective family problems, everyone was so busy and so financially committed with all of the extra expense, our wedding suddenly didn't feature at all. We obviously wouldn't be getting any help or support with anything.

We had booked the wedding at John's family village church, which was what his mother wanted, and the reception was to be over the road at the restaurant – both venues were exactly where Celia had had her special day, now a memory that could only reduce her to a sobbing wreck. All I heard from John's family was, "Poor Celia, how will she cope, having to sit through a wedding in the same place as she was married, when she was so happy…"

But Celia was coping very well, thank you, courtesy

of good old Sandra. When I met Celia for the first time, I did feel for her, although I couldn't possibly tell her we had marital disaster in common, but I was struck by seeing the same hardness that Sandra wore like a badge of honour. There was no human warmth at all, and Celia seemed to be angry, and even jealous, that we were about to be married while she was suffering so much. She said the last thing she wanted right now was to attend a wedding.

It saddened me greatly that now both families were so taken up with serious issues, they had no time or energy to be happy about our big day. I started to feel that sense of isolation creep over me again, and, of course, John was leaving everything to me.

It may have been a completely different time and different circumstances, but I was, once more, on my own.

Chapter 10: The Big Bad Day

I was such a different person back then. I know now that, when something in life makes you feel uncomfortable, it's because it's wrong for you and you need to make changes. But there I was, about as far from the happy, floating-on-air bride-to-be as I could get, and yet I kept telling myself everything was going to be fine.

John had been complaining about living at my house, and wanting me to move to his place in the village. His house was bigger, it had a good-sized garden, it was close to his family, where his roots were.

"After all," he reasoned with me, "when we do have children they'll have a big garden to play in and plenty of space around the house – and village life is much safer for kids."

I couldn't really argue, but I didn't relish the idea of moving to the other side of town, living so close to his mother and sister when they obviously didn't want to have anything to do with me. But it wasn't just about me now, it was about the two of us and our future family, so it did make sense. As I was packing my boxes, I knew I should be feeling excited, keen to start my new life, but I couldn't shake off the doubt about what lay ahead.

While I busied myself with decorating the rooms in John's house to make it more homely, my lovely little house, where I had felt at peace with myself for the first time, was rented out. It saddened me that strangers would be living there and, for a second, I felt uncomfortable with all of the changes that were happening, but I shook this off, putting it down to pre-wedding nerves.

And then came the day. Lovely, bright, sunny day. And my own personal sunshine, my Grandma, came to be with me at the house while I was getting ready. My dress was cream, not white, because it seemed to be the right thing to do. The excitement I should have been feeling was replaced by a sense of acceptance and I just wanted the day to be over, then I could get on with being John's wife and – hopefully – have our children.

In church, you could cut the atmosphere with a knife. John's family on the one side, mine on the other, each with a sister carrying a heavy heart and each struggling with their recent family upheaval, lives that had been torn apart and with young children involved. You couldn't ignore the gloom that hung over the ceremony, and I was having my own struggle, trying to appear as the blushing bride, while inwardly wishing we weren't here – not here, not now, not with these unhappy people. I had tried to please everyone and ended up pleasing no-one.

The reception could have been better. It was a sit-down meal so the mood was more obvious. Glancing at the guests, I could see the miserable faces of some people who so clearly didn't want to be there.

This whole day was blighted by things that were way beyond my control. Sandra was knocking back the whisky, so my dad wasn't going to bother making conversation with her; the speeches were dry and formal, no real attempt at humour in case anyone would get upset; and the families didn't know each other and made absolutely no effort to mingle. I silently thanked my lucky stars that we weren't having an evening 'do' and by four o'clock in the afternoon it was over, done, finished. The relief was enormous. John had been in his silly 'fun' mood the whole time, so at least this difficult day wasn't made any worse.

Barbados, on the other hand, was just what the doctor ordered, truly amazing, even if it was only for a one-week honeymoon. I was much happier, now it was just the two of us and we were *finally* trying to make a baby.

Back in the village, place of my new home and harsh reality, my mother-in-law couldn't find a single good word to say about the wedding, and she made her views crystal clear. She pointed out the things I hadn't done, the things I'd forgotten to do, what I should have done, and what was wrong with the things I had done – and she showed no mercy, pulled no punches.

According to her, everything had been wrong. Why had I bothered trying to please her, because I knew that would always be an impossibility for me. Celia, of course, had the same criticisms as her mother.

This was the part I'd known would present problems for me: I was living so close to the people who made it abundantly clear that they had no time for me, that they never agreed with anything I said or did, and that this would never change. Sandra remained aloof, while Celia was bitter because she was alone while I was the happy new bride. That's how she saw me, anyway.

I should have known better by now, but I mentioned to John that I was unhappy with this constant rejection and criticism from his family, and he wouldn't hear a word of it.

"It's all in your head! I have no idea why you keep saying these things... what's wrong with you? Just because your own mother's dead, don't take it out on mine! You're just jealous!"

To be painfully honest, I did wonder if he could be right, even if he could have found a better way to say it! I took a mental step back and looked at the situation. I could see the bond between Sandra and Celia, a mother-daughter thing that I'd missed out on for so long. Was I jealous, or was it really them making me feel pushed out? Maybe that's how mothers and their girls were, with their special cosy little togetherness that excluded everything else. I had no way of knowing.

Sandra's sitting-room was adorned with photos of

Celia and her children. The one single photo from our wedding that she'd ordered was the smallest size available and was almost hidden from view, high up on a shelf. Trying a bit of a different tack, I made a joke of this with John. "I see your mum didn't like our choice of photographer – she's put our wedding photo out of sight!" I even laughed aloud.

"That's nonsense! You always over-think everything, you're so stupid. Don't judge my family – go and judge your own. Leave mine out of it!" He wouldn't even try to understand my point of view, he just automatically took his mother's side over everything.

John had got me to move to his side of town, fifteen miles from where my dad and Shirley lived, and anyway, they were busy with their children, their own life. His mother was never going to let me in, accept me as part of the family, and my new husband didn't want to know how I felt about anything. Didn't care.

Things weren't looking very good. But, a couple of months after the wedding, I was pregnant! I was having a baby! At last! Having children was the one thing I knew could fill the painful void that had crept into my life and very nearly taken over.

Chapter 11: A Child is Born

I actually punched the air and shouted, "How wonderful! I'm pregnant!" in my own very private celebration. After a total of four separate pregnancy tests, I had finally allowed myself to believe it and now I was overflowing with joy and happiness. The weight of the guilt I'd been carrying since that awful experience of the abortion had made me consider that perhaps I wouldn't be able to conceive again after that. You know, as a punishment for what I'd done. But life was apparently not judging me quite so harshly.

My husband, however, managed to disappoint me once more. Disappoint and confuse. Having used the argument that our future children would be happier in his house than in mine, which made me believe he was looking forward to us having our own family, his reaction – or lack of it – to the announcement was astonishing.

"That's good." His total contribution. No big grin, no happy face, no apparent pleasure and definitely no celebration. The man was like a machine.

When I'd given in to John's cajoling over living in the village, he had promised me that one day in our future we would move to somewhere new, and I'd been hanging on to that light on the horizon ever since. It was what enabled me to tolerate the black clouds of doom and gloom that were blown my way every day from the house across the road.

Although incredibly happy with my soon-to-be baby, the pregnancy itself caused me constant and severe sickness, all through the term, and John gave me no sympathy, no support, no comfort – nothing. All I got was scorn and derision.

"How come millions of women all over the world have babies every day? If it was that bad, they wouldn't would they?"

And off he'd go, to work, and he wouldn't reappear until about eight in the evening, by which time I'd had the day from hell, hanging over the toilet, heaving and throwing up. But he'd still expect his dinner on the table and he never once made any effort to cook or even to give me a hand.

I heard from other women how their men had doted on them through their pregnancy, couldn't do enough for them, and I wondered why John wasn't showing the slightest sign of even helping me out, let alone any doting. I went for all of my scans on my own, I visited the labour ward on my own; it was as though I didn't have a husband. Ever the optimist, I thought John would change when the baby came, that he would suddenly feel something good and loving for me and our new child. Wrong again.

We couldn't even buy the pram without another battle. I did manage to get the one I wanted, but John came home the next day in a complete rage, shouting about my dad, saying he should have paid for the pram and what a "mean bastard" he was.

My labour pains began in the evening and John took me to the hospital, where they told him he might as well go home because I probably wouldn't give birth until the next day. He didn't need telling twice. I spent a sleepless night in pain and then the contractions came, and my only company was a nurse who I didn't know. John did make it back for the actual birth.

And then, there he was, our little boy, baby David John. I was overwhelmed with pride and love, and it was so intensely emotional, all I could do was cry. The bond I felt with this little person from the second he appeared was so immense, so powerful, it engulfed me. And he was a beautiful baby, too. John had barely set eyes on his new son before he announced he was off to work! The nursing staff were amazed, and not impressed. The next time I saw him was at nine that night, after he'd had dinner – at his mother's!

When he did eventually turn up, he had a gift for me. A gold necklace. But I didn't want jewellery, I wanted him to show some affection towards me and our new baby, to be excited at the arrival of our first child, to show me he was happy with his new little family. He really didn't understand why I wasn't thrilled with the necklace. He just didn't get it.

I took our little boy home, still bursting with joy and a new feeling that was growing in me – I felt incredibly protective of this amazing tiny person. Both my family and John's were busy with their first grandchildren and there was no support coming my way, plus John didn't even suggest taking any time off work, so I just got on with my new role. I was a mum, a happy and very proud new mum. Nothing could change how I felt about that.

John never once offered to do a feed or change a nappy, and when he saw me looking tired all I got was "Why are you so tired all the time? Other women can cope." I would reply with "Well, maybe other women have husbands who help with the new baby duties." And John would tell me to get my "mean bastard" dad to help out, and so it went, on and on. I missed my mum all the more. She would have been here, helping out, letting me get some rest, giving me support and advice. She would have made this a time for love and happiness, not harsh words and rejection.

When David was three months old, I told John I'd like to have him christened. We'd saved the top tier from our wedding cake specially for this occasion, and I wanted my baby christened with God's blessing – it was something I felt strongly about because that's how I'd been brought up. John, of course, had to throw a spanner into the works and this time it was his announcement that my dad couldn't come to the christening. So my whole family wouldn't be invited.

They never knew about it.

In the church, it was just us, his parents and his sister, still with the scowling face (or maybe that was just when I was around). So John had got his own way again. His way or no way.

Chapter 12: The Three of Us

Life rolled on in our dysfunctional fashion. Each morning, John would go off to work and we'd have no contact until he reappeared in the early evening, when he would have his dinner, spend some time being silly with little David, and then the rest of the evening was taken up with me as his audience, hearing all about his day at work. Never once did he ask what sort of day I'd had, or what I'd been doing. I was completely irrelevant.

I decided I'd like to start work but John always said no, he felt my place was at home with the baby. I didn't *need* to work, as I was getting the rent from my house and there was the family allowance, plus John would leave cash for me to pay for shopping. We never went without.

David had his share of medical problems as time went by, with repeated ear infections, sometimes he'd have febrile convulsions, and he suffered with asthma. John's mother, ever the doting grandmother (joke), showed not the slightest sympathy. In her opinion, nothing could be anywhere near as bad as when her precious little John had his arm infection, of course. What I couldn't tolerate was her smoking around David, when she was fully aware of his asthma. I asked her if she'd mind not having a cigarette whenever I took him to see her. The reply was unbelievable.

"This is *my* house, Paula. You can't tell me what to do."

And, when I mentioned this to John, he shrugged it off and stuck up for his mother.

"She's right. It's her house. Stop creating problems."

There was only one thing I could do, and so I stopped taking David to see his grandmother. She didn't bother coming over to us, either. The situation wasn't good.

I did want another child, a brother or sister for David – a proper little family. We went away on holiday and when we came home I was pregnant. I was thrilled, overjoyed, and my husband was, as ever, his usual unemotional self. He would never be any different, and I couldn't change that, but his increasingly insulting and demeaning comments were starting to wear me down.

"You've let yourself go. Other women aren't like you."

Or, "Why can't you just be *normal?*"

"But I *am normal!*" I would try to make the point, but it fell on deaf ears. It was useless to attempt to defend myself against his verbal abuse.

The only family support I had was from two aunts on my mum's side of the family, but I never told them how my life really was. I didn't tell anybody. I just kept up the appearance of everything being OK, I went to the playgroups, did the shopping, cooked meals and carried on. I felt that John and I were worlds apart, different planets really, and I couldn't talk to him about anything real, anything that wasn't *his* work, *his* family, *his* world. Whenever I had tried to communicate with him on an intimate level, I was shrugged off with some curt insult. And everything that went wrong was always my fault, it was all down to me and my family – even though we never saw them and they'd done nothing wrong.

The new pregnancy, just like with David, made me very sick right through the full term and, as I had expected, John offered me no support, no help, no sympathy, even though it was obvious I was getting worse as the months passed by, and at around thirty-four weeks I was beginning to show signs of pre-eclampsia, with high blood pressure, protein in the wee, swelling and constant tiredness.

We called in to see John's parents. His dad, the lovely Eric, had told Sandra not to smoke! I was explaining to her that I might have to have the baby early as I was developing pre-eclampsia. Without so much as looking in my direction, she announced that she was going to Tenerife in two weeks with Celia and her children. Eric wasn't going. He was sick of his controlling shrew of a wife and needed a break from her, and, being the good person he was, he had concerns about our baby.

I asked Sandra if she would still be going away if I were her daughter in this condition.

"Well, you're not my daughter!"

"No, I'm not, but this is your grandchild!" I couldn't help myself. Picking David up, I left.

It didn't help that my family weren't exactly rallying round, so John could no doubt feel justified in his criticisms.

"Your own family aren't bothered about you so stop having a go at mine! Why d'you need to be propped up all the time?"

The next day, I was admitted to hospital, which didn't surprise me as the hassles with John and his mother couldn't have done anything to improve my blood pressure. With no-one to look after little David, we had no choice but to hire a nanny, which I really wasn't happy with, but she brought him to see me every day while John was at work. After two weeks of bed rest, the decision was made to induce the birth. A new baby girl! Little Alice Faye was so tiny, and so pretty! Just as with David's birth, I was full of love and joy, I had two beautiful children, such a special gift.

Sandra had just flown out to Tenerife and so missed the happy event, but Eric came to see his new granddaughter and he fell in love with her. John stayed away most of the time, of course. Alice and I were in recovery and had been moved into a side room; I was still swollen up and my blood pressure was being monitored every two hours, while little Alice was jaundiced and lay under an ultra-violet lamp.

I couldn't understand why my family weren't coming to visit. Days passed by, and nothing. I was having to ask other people's visitors to fetch things from the hospital shop for me and the baby. My only regular visitor was the nanny with little David. Until one night, it must have been about ten o'clock and I was asleep, when a nurse appeared and told me I had a visitor.

"Who is it?"

"It's your dad."

My relief was overwhelming and I burst into tears. "Why haven't you been to see me, Dad?" I sobbed.

His words knocked the breath out of me. "Because we're so scared of John."

I'd been seriously ill and little Alice was having her own problems, and yet my own dad hadn't felt he could come to see us. Dad had purposely turned up later in the evening so that he wouldn't bump into John, because he was so worried. I didn't get it. Why were they all frightened of John? Had he perhaps threatened them in some way? But I was too poorly to start going into the deeper issues of John and families. I didn't ask, I just admired the little red dress Dad and Shirley had bought for my new baby. But I was devastated that now it appeared John had somehow separated me from my family.

How on earth, I asked myself, could we ever have a happy family life together, when I was constantly battling with John's mother and sister, and now I knew my relatives were staying away because they feared my husband, plus there was the never-ending private war between me and him. But my over-riding feeling was that I needed to keep the marriage together in order to have any chance of a decent family life, like the one I'd had. I simply couldn't fail my two wonderful children, now that I'd been blessed with them.

A few days later, Alice and I were allowed to go home. John went to work, the nanny left, and it was just me and the children. Sandra came to visit, with Celia and her two. They had me waiting on them hand and foot, talking constantly about how amazing the holiday was, never once asking how I was, or how Alice was doing, and Sandra just couldn't resist making a huge point of putting Celia's daughter on her lap and saying, "There'll only ever be one granddaughter for me and that's my precious Lorna." Then they got up and went home, leaving me to clear up the mess they had all made.

So, there I stayed, in John's village, in his house, opposite his spiteful mother and sister, and without any of my own family around. He'd got me where he wanted. I was isolated.

We had Alice's christening and, just as with David's, my family weren't invited and didn't even know about it. And, having agreed it would just be the two of us with the children, John invited his mother, his dad and Celia.

Always, always his own way.

Chapter 13: Confusion and Questions

John hated my family, there was no doubt about that, and now I knew my family were afraid of him. But why? With no-one explaining anything to me, and no-one close to confide in, to talk things through, I ,was beginning to have a lot of questions. Who was right and who was in the wrong here? Who was causing which issues? Who was really at fault? Could I be wrong? I was so confused.

Very, very confused...

The main source of my confusion was John himself. Why did he have to keep veering between 'Nice John', the person we loved and had good times with, and the other John, who shouted and swore and hit out, and generally made life a misery? What was it that made him switch like that all the time? Like so many people, I always hoped that his good side would eventually take over and he'd have no reason to turn into the nasty, vile person he could so easily become. He really was a lovely husband and father at times, laughing and playing, having fun, but – without any warning and for absolutely no apparent reason – something must have snapped inside his head and he would change in such a drastic way, in a single instant.

When he was being his amiable self, I really loved him and I so desperately wanted us to be happy together. I wished something would give me a clue, an insight, into what caused this sudden change of character. Then, maybe, I could do something about it... but I was at a loss.

When Alice was a few months old, we all went to visit John's mother and that's when I found out she had sold all of the children's toys and equipment that had been kept at her place – knowing that we could have made good use of everything. She was making the point that she was *not* going to be looking after our children. Not ever.

As well as being father and son, Eric and John were business partners and I knew they were close. Eric was diagnosed with bowel cancer and, sadly, it was untreatable. They told him he only had a matter of months to live. David was three and Alice only six months old. It hit us all really hard.

Something made John spring into action at the news, wanting to get one particular aspect of our life sorted before his dad died. The agenda was getting us moved into the 'dream house' where Eric had apparently always thought John should live. It was a big old rambling place, a manor house, all sandstone and arched windows, set in a really lovely big piece of land, it had gardens with tall trees and lawns... it would have been my dream home, too, were it not for one small point. It was still in the same village, still where John wanted to be, still on his mother's doorstep.

One snag was that I had to sell my house to help fund the new place. That meant losing my bit of financial independence, which I have to say had always felt like a safety net, but I didn't really mind because this move seemed to have given John something to focus on apart from work – a project – and we were making all sorts of plans to do the place up and make it *ours*. I took this as a positive sign and quietly prayed that perhaps we'd reached some kind of turning-point.

We'd barely got moved in when John came steaming in from work in the most foul, aggressive mood, and he was clutching some paperwork. He slammed the documents down on the kitchen table and, with a face like thunder, he demanded, "Here, sign this!"

"What is it?"

"Don't ask! Just sign it!" His voice was getting louder and I could see the anger building in him, but I knew the sheer stupidity of signing anything without checking it first. Like a normal person would. I said I'd sign it if he would just please tell me what it was for. Grabbing hold of my arms and twisting them, so that I yelped in pain, he put his face right up to mine and hissed at me, "You'll sign or I'll make your life very difficult". All I could see from the top sheet of paper was that it was from the bank, then I was shoved down into a chair next to the table.

"Sign it, you bitch! You don't need to read it!"

I glanced towards where the children were playing together, and he read my mind.

"Carry on like this and you'll upset the kids – is that what you want? Is it?"

They had noticed things weren't right and they were both looking up at their daddy with big innocent eyes. I didn't want them to witness anything else. I took the pen he was jabbing towards my face and I signed. All I could hope was that it was something sensible, but if that was so, why couldn't he just ask me properly, in a normal manner, instead of creating such a scene? It was worrying.

Eric passed away, and I was sad to lose him.

John's mood swings seemed to get worse. In the space of a few hours, he could subject me to his verbal attacks of vile insults and degradation, physical violence, threats and all sorts of put-downs, then go to work and come home later with a little-boy grin spread across his face, pat me on the behind and tell me if I played my cards right, this could be my lucky night. When he was like this – playful and silly, with not a scrap of malice in him, I'd look at him and think, "Why can't you be this person all the time? Why do you have to keep changing into that awful person who hates the world and its dog?" But I never got an answer.

Alice was getting towards her second birthday when John suggested it might be a good time for me to start working again, and I agreed straight away. I'd lost so much of myself by being separated from my folks and giving up my career to be a wife and mother, being pushed away by his mother all the time and with the constant battles with him, I had little or no confidence and I knew I needed to build some independence, regain my former strength of character. I was looking forward to getting back into nursing. But John had other plans. I should have guessed.

One evening, we were sitting out in the garden and John had poured me several glasses of wine. He was in a lovely mood and was obviously excited about something.

"You can be my secretary!"

At first, I couldn't think of anything worse, but he sold the idea to me by adding that I could work at home, I could take any amount of time off if the children were ill or needed me, we could take holidays whenever we liked, and it would only be for about fifteen hours a week or so, which I could easily fit around school runs and so on. Now, it sounded like every woman's perfect job! So we made it official and I started work.

How could I not have seen what was coming? He was just the same with work as he was with everything else, constantly belittling everything I did, shouting and telling me I'd got it all wrong, telling me how stupid I was... even once tipping me right off my chair! His previous secretary had left. I wonder why.

I stuck it for a while, but I was turning to a wine bottle most evenings after putting the children to bed, just to numb the anxiety, the worry, the – let's face it, the bloody depression that he could so easily drown me in.

By now, my family never came near and I would meet them secretly for coffee in town while John was at work, always making sure I was back home, with dinner ready, before he came in. I'd lie about where I'd been. "Oh, just getting a few bits in town that we can't get in the village. Nothing special."

I was putting weight on at a rather alarming rate, what with the wine and now the comfort eating as well. My feeling of isolation was very powerful and I couldn't shake it off, even when I was with the children. Knowing my life was a sham, if you like, with everything looking wonderful on the outside but on the inside like an apple with a rotten core. People used to comment on how lucky we were – lovely children, beautiful home, great holidays, expensive cars, our own business and so on. But all of that doesn't make you happy.

We still went on holidays, as a family now. But what that meant was, I would look after the children while John would go off somewhere, every night without fail, and he'd come back around three or four the next morning, not really drunk but making enough noise to disturb everyone. The children would be up bright and early, wanting Daddy to take them down to the pool with their inflatable dolphins, but he'd roll over and ignore us all. We were a nuisance.

Sometimes he'd join us for breakfast, but he wasn't

really *with us*: as he'd toy with his food or fiddle about on his mobile phone, I'd look around the dining room at other families, and I'd wonder if this was how we all were. Was this normal life? Had these other husbands all been out for most of the night while the women stayed in their hotel room with the children?

"Why can't you just be a normal wife and respect your husband?" he'd say, and I did begin to wonder, to question myself. Was I really not normal? Is that what made him so cross all the time? Was it really my fault? Was I the cause of all this unhappiness?

Then I'd see him playing in the water with the children, as if nothing was wrong, like always.

Chapter 14: Merry Monopoly

Family life as we knew it became the norm, even though, being totally honest with myself, the life we were living was far from 'normal'.

It almost made me feel I had become two different people, especially when I was reminded of how others saw us – successful, enjoying the good life, happy family, and so on. The company had grown to a much higher level now, with John and his amazing business brain adding other lucrative aspects to the existing portfolio. And yes, we reaped the benefits – but only in material terms, and that doesn't buy happiness.

All I had to do was make sure John remained as calm as possible, keep my head down and carry on with the charade, make it appear that everything in our garden was rosy – just like being back in church, where it was all about how things appeared. That was the most important thing to him, that none of what we experienced at his hands leaked out to the world at large.

I honestly believed I could do this, but I was being incredibly naïve, of course, because people like John can't remain in a calm state for too long, they just have to snap, they have to become aggressive and violent, become your worst nightmare, again.

It happened while we were getting ready for the new day ahead, with John in the *en suite*, brushing his teeth, and me needing to get the children off to nursery and infant school. The garage key was in John's sweatshirt pocket, so I reached in as he was leaning over the hand basin. I must have startled him and he swung round quickly, accidentally letting his toothbrush knock against his (overly sensitive) teeth. That flicked his switch and he was in angry mode in an instant.

Shoving me heavily to the floor and banging my head on the bath panel, he started shouting and swearing loudly, telling his non-existent audience what a low-life I was. Then, as his tirade grew louder and more threatening, I was dragged by my hair out into the hallway, where he began kicking me, every assault aimed at my side and each one pushing me up against the skirting board. All I could do was curl up as tightly as I could until he ran out of steam.

"You're abnormal, woman! You're filth! Nobody knows what I have to put up with!" One almighty final kick, this time to my head, sent my nose hard into the solid wood. Agonising pain seared through my face, stabbing at my skull.

Like a wounded animal too injured to run, I just lay there. The children were still downstairs, finishing their breakfast, and – hopefully – oblivious to the racket upstairs because the kitchen radio was on. But John couldn't even allow them that. He had to announce his latest outburst, which, as usual, was all my fault.

"Your stupid mother's really gone and done it now!" he shouted to them. "I've got to do something about her – she's completely mad!"

With that, he left.

Although I barely had the energy to move, the children had to get to school, and then I could have the house to myself to clean up properly and nurse my injuries. Somehow, I got us all into the car and drove the couple of miles round trip. I thought David and Alice were unaware of this latest attack, but then David's little voice came from the back seat. "Daddy is very naughty, isn't he, Mummy?"

I prayed that he wouldn't tell his teachers and I was, once again, utterly ashamed.

Back in the sanctuary of the empty house, I sat by the fire, cradling a big mug of tea in both hands, aware that bruises were starting to come out on my face, my side, arms and legs, and I felt shaky and dazed. I tried to think.

Maybe it was the shock, but a decision began to take shape, and it felt right. I needed this incident to go on record, I needed John to be held to account – in whatever way that could be – and he really should be told in no uncertain terms that what he was doing was *not* acceptable, by any standards.

Clambering gingerly into the car and trying to

avoid knocking any of my injured areas, I drove to the police station, feeling like a real victim of domestic abuse – but I suppose that's exactly what I was. The police took me seriously and made notes as I recounted the awful scenario. When they asked if there was anyone they could call for me, I insisted that wasn't necessary: I couldn't stand the thought of anyone finding out.

That was it. They told me they'd sort it out and off I went, back home again.

That afternoon, John came home early. The police had been in touch and wanted to speak to him, which had thrown him into a real state of panic. I enjoyed seeing him worried about what would happen, seeing him squirm. It was nothing compared to what he did to me.

"Please, please drop these charges, Paula?" He was actually pleading with me! My, how easily the tables can be turned.

"My reputation will be destroyed, no-one will do business with me... we'll lose everything! Our family will be finished!"

As soon as I heard his words, I felt a terrible pang of guilt for reporting him. I saw that I had acted rather rashly – after all, I didn't want to be in the local papers, labelled as a battered wife... the children labelled as victims of domestic abuse! God, no! Why on earth did I go to the police? I was questioning myself, and all my resolve of earlier that day was gone.

Back at the station for the second time that day, I

hung my head and explained that I wanted to drop the charges. The police were (and still are) so used to this, because most women who are eventually driven to reporting domestic abuse refuse to carry on with the case, once the errant husband has shown them his 'nice' side again, apologised, promised everything will be fine. They were disappointed at my decision, but my mind was made up – and John was waiting in the car outside.

"Good girl," he said, without looking at me, "and don't ever do that again." Then he dropped me back at the house and went off to work.

Later, at the school, one of the other mothers did notice some of my bruises, and asked what on earth I'd been up to. I told her the "I was up a ladder, doing some decorating, and fell off" story. I think she believed me. Why shouldn't she?

Coming home later, John was in a good mood and talked about his day at work, asked what was for dinner, and generally behaved as if nothing had happened. Everything was swept under the carpet.

I took solace in a bottle of wine, as I always did these days. It seemed to be my only form of escape. I had no money, no job, no support, nowhere to run, and I had a husband who beat me black and blue and then acted as if everything was fine.

There simply was no escape for me and the children. What was the alternative to staying? Life as a single parent? My desperation to hold the family together wouldn't allow me to consider that, and the very idea of restricted access visits and my children having step-parents and step-siblings was, for me, a bridge too far.

Soon, it was Christmas again. I more or less knew how it would pan out, with John doing his own thing down the pub on Christmas Eve, either with a business contact or someone he regarded as a friend. I knew that some local people would ask him why he never took his wife out with him, but it didn't matter to me any longer. I actually appreciated the break from him and his two personalities. His unpredictability was all too stressful.

John never wanted to get out of bed on Christmas Day, and if the children and I tried to get him to come and join us, he would become angry, his hangover from the night before clinging desperately to the pillow. It would have been easier to leave him there, but I wanted the children to have both parents around them on this special day – just like it had been for me all those years ago.

When the children eventually managed to get their father downstairs, he would sit there, huddled in his dressing-gown, in this blank, almost comatose state, not moving, not speaking, and all of the fun and glee we'd been having would evaporate and disappear into John's personal cloud of gloom.

Every now and then, he would throw out a few nasty comments, most of which would be targeted towards me and my family. "Is that all they've bought you? See, kids – that's how little your mother's family think of you!"

The same every year, he just couldn't resist spoiling

everything, and he never once considered how his vile words were affecting the children.

"Oh, now, look what *my* mother's bought you! Now, that's a proper present, kids! She's your lovely kind granny, not like those fucking peasant relatives of your mother's!"

I found this particular criticism incredibly odd because, whenever she thought a gift was required, Celia would give me the most ridiculous things: once it was a bunch of dead flowers, there was a bag of broken biscuits, self-help books, and she would give the children a packet of sweets from the Pound Shop!

And then, regardless of what I did to try to change this ridiculous routine, came the highlight of the day, when John's mother and sister would come over for Christmas dinner. If ever a tradition had been designed with the sole intent of demeaning, demoralising and degrading a human being, this was it. I would wait on them hand and foot, and they would be rude to me, insult me, make fun of me...

Of course, no matter how my witty responses to their ignorance would pile up inside my head, I couldn't say a single word, otherwise I would make things worse for myself. I knew not to tempt Fate.

And so, the day would pass with the children wishing they were somewhere else, me keeping my mouth shut and playing chief cook and bottle washer, and John and his family displaying their usual sick, twisted and bitter characters. John hated seeing people having fun, enjoying a good time, and I could see where he had got that from!

Because we were banned from singing, dancing, playing games, reading stories, taking photos or family videos, and basically everything normal folk did for fun, we would end up playing Monopoly because, according to John, that was 'normal' and for people who had a 'proper upbringing'.

And so, Monopoly it was, again. It was John's way or woe betide you.

Chapter 15: Daddy's on the TV

One particularly beautiful summer's day, I thought how nice it would be to take the children to the zoo. John had told me he would be gone for the whole day, so I decided it would be safe to take my two little nephews along with us, and he wouldn't find out.

With a tasty picnic made and packed in the car boot, and David and Alice keen to go, we set off in the sunshine, singing along to the radio. A happy start to a lovely day – or so I thought.

Arriving at Dad's, we picked the boys up and got them settled in the car, then I headed in the direction of the zoo. Suddenly, I realised I had left our guinea pig in his pen while I cleaned out the hutch, and I had forgotten to pop him back inside. This heat would be too much for the poor little thing, and there was no shade or water in the pen, so I did a bit of a detour back to the house.

Turning into the drive, my heart sank when I saw John's car parked by the house. Panic set in. Quickly as

I could, I sorted the guinea pig and popped into the hallway, forcing a smile and trying to appear calm, but wondering what on earth I could say to John.

"Where are the kids?" he was frowning, and that was always a bad sign.

"Oh, they're in the car... we're going out for the day as it's such nice weather."

"Who with?" It was as if he could read my mind, and that made me even more nervous, but, before I could reply, he was marching off towards my car. Then he saw the boys.

"Where are you going?" he demanded.

The little chorus of delighted voices would charm anyone – except John. "To the zoo! We're going to see the animals!"

I knew what was coming, and I was filled with dread yet again as he swung round towards me.

"Taking your filthy lot out on my cash! You're all filthy scroungers, the lot of you! I'm not paying for some other bastard kids!"

He was livid, out of control. He started to walk back into the house and I followed, trying to reason with him. "But I've promised David and Alice, and they are really looking forward to it..."

John turned on me, his face dark red, eyes bulging, and screamed at me, "You're not going to any bloody zoo!" and with that, he kicked me. He was wearing work boots with metal toe-caps, and the sudden pain shocked me, dropping me to the floor in a heap. My leg was on fire, I couldn't breathe. I thought I would pass out, and there was no way I could stand up.

I couldn't drive now. John had won again. Not only was driving out of the question, but I knew I should get to A & E for an X-ray. My leg felt as if something was broken and the pain was awful. I was crying, sobbing, helpless. He stood there, looking down at me, and he smirked.

"Well, now you won't be taking that lot to the zoo, will you?" and he walked away.

My nephews came running into the house, and I had to think quickly, despite the pain. I told them I'd had an accident with the guinea pig hutch and it had fallen on my leg, so I wouldn't be able to drive to the zoo. Their little faces were a picture of disappointment, and all I could do was promise we'd go another day.

We had our picnic in the garden and later I sent the boys home in a taxi. That was such a very sad day.

Once I'd got David and Alice tucked up in bed, I went to the hospital. John couldn't care less; he said it was my fault for going behind his back.

The X-ray showed no actual break, thank heaven, but the bone was chipped and the whole lower leg was badly swollen and bruised all over. The doctor asked me how it had happened, and I told him the truth. I did stress that I wouldn't be pressing charges and I didn't want it to go any further. I was still terrified that anything I tried to do would bring down the business and leave us all homeless and with nothing. It didn't matter for myself, but I couldn't do that to the children.

Under the pretence of the guinea pig hutch

accident, I hobbled around for weeks. There was never any comeback from what I'd told the doctor, for which I was grateful.

But John was getting more and more vicious, more evil in his outbursts, more easily angered, and I knew that the more he got away with, the worse he became.

A few weeks after that hideous time, a new TV set arrived to replace the old one in the lounge. Wide screen, wrap-around sound, top of the range (of course), and the children were delighted. The old set wasn't worth anything and I decided it would be nice to give it to Dad so the boys could use it.

John went berserk. The poor old TV was hurled out on to the drive, smashed to pieces, and then he walked all over the broken bits, so the pieces kept getting smaller and making more of a mess. As he trampled around, the sounds of breaking glass and plastic cracking against the gravel, he was shouting aloud, "Now your filthy family can have it!" Then he kicked it all around the driveway.

Not content with this insane and totally unnecessary behaviour, he lunged at me and grabbed my arms, squeezing my flesh until his fingers were almost cutting into my skin. "Now I hope you've learned your lesson!"

Then I was shoved into the front porch, my face pressed against the window, my mouth so firmly on the glass I feared it would break. I could barely breathe, and now John's hand was clutching my throat and he was squeezing, choking the life out of me.

"What did I just say?" he snarled.

I had no option but to say what he wanted to hear. "I've learned my lesson, John... please let me go..." I was gasping for air.

"I hope so, you filthy peasant!" he spat the words at the back of my head and then threw me out on to the gravel drive, where I landed in a heap, the grit grazing my knees and elbows.

My knees were skinned and bleeding, I was coughing to get my breath and feeling about as low as I could get without actually giving up altogether.

Picking myself up like some discarded rag doll, I staggered into the kitchen to get a drink of water, and I found the children there. They had seen everything through the window. I was overwhelmed with sadness for them.

Sending the children to play in the garden, I could see John, still stomping on the now unrecognisable TV set, and I thought how he reminded me of Rumpelstiltskin from the fairy tale, who stamped his feet so much when he was angry, he made a hole in the ground and fell into it, never to be seen again. Oh, if only.

"Look what my mad wife has done! She's damaged! She needs help!" He couldn't stop. I was certain the neighbours would hear his ranting and see what he was doing, and he wasn't calming down – in fact, he seemed to be getting more and more furious. I suddenly had the most awful feeling that things were going to get even worse.

Fear took over. I ran to the door and bolted it. John heard the sound of the metal bolt and started banging on the door as hard as he could, shouting, "Let me in, you filthy pig of a woman! This is *my* house, not yours!" Then he started kicking the door, but I couldn't let him in – I really thought he might kill us all this time, he was so oblivious to reality, so consumed in his own anger, his hatred of everything and everyone.

Then it struck me – the children were still playing in the garden. Oh, dear God, I had to act fast. John was shouting to them, "Kids! Come here! Your mad mother has locked us all out!"

I could see both David and Alice were beginning to feel scared. I called to David, "No, David! You and Alice come inside quickly! Daddy's in a very bad mood!"

I managed to get them both inside the house, but we only just made it as John had clambered over the side gate and was now banging his fists on the lounge window. I was terrified, and not just for myself this time.

"Fucking lazy bitch! David, please let me in?" As he shouted, David began making his way towards the window, and it was clear that he was going to let John in. He was too young to have any understanding of what was really going on, thankfully.

I just got hold of his hand in time and ran towards the playroom with him and Alice. Once inside, I locked the door and told the children to play with their toys. I knew we were really in big trouble.

There was the loud sound of glass shattering. John had taken one of his boots off and smashed the window, then he reached inside and unfastened the handle. What now?

I ran upstairs as fast as I could, at the same time being terrified that the children were downstairs in the playroom. I heard John run upstairs, muttering under his breath about how mad I was. My heart was pounding so badly, I felt I'd pass out. But I had to get to the bathroom – the door had a proper lock on it...

Hands grabbed at my ankles and I was dragged to the floor. He was like a man possessed. Throwing me over on to my back, he cleared his throat and spat in my face, disgusting phlegm on my skin, my mouth. He was screaming, his face touching mine now, "Fat filthy bitch! Who'd want *you*? You're a total loser! You've got no respect for me! Scrounging, abnormal woman! Why can't you be normal, like other women?"

He reached out and took hold of Alice's music stand, smashing it down hard on me. My wrist was bleeding. I couldn't take much more. My fear for the children was pounding in my head. They were calling for me.

John gave one final almighty kick to my leg. The same pain as last time shot through my calf, seared up into my thigh. It was agony.

Suddenly, for no reason, he stood up and walked downstairs. I heard him unlock the playroom door. "Hi, kids! I've had to tell your mum off – she's been a bit naughty today, but she's OK now, she's learned her lesson!"

Then, to my horror, he said, "Why don't we go visit Granny while your mum has a bit of a rest? She's looking very tired these days but I don't know why – she doesn't do anything all day!"

The bathroom mirror was not my friend that day, as I rinsed off the spit that always made me feel more disgusted than any of John's other dreadful ways. I hated him. He was a monster. We couldn't go on living like this, because something terrible would happen, I was sure of it. And now he was involving the children in his mad games, and I couldn't allow that.

I dialled 999. Once again, I was telling the police about the domestic abuse I was experiencing. They were at the house inside of three minutes.

John was stunned. He couldn't believe it. I was thrown by how nice the police were to him, but it was their tactic to keep him calm until they got him to the station.

The children cuddled up with me on the settee. They were very confused. One of the police officers sat down and told me, "He's gone to the police station now." His voice was very kind, understanding.

I left the children where they were and beckoned to him to follow me into the kitchen. "Your husband isn't a nice person at all, is he? Why are you with him?"

I stood there, lost for any words. I shook my head. Life was a mess.

And now, social services were involved. Just what I had tried so hard to avoid.

Chapter 16: Turning the Tables

The situation had suddenly escalated and was spiralling out of control, or so it felt. Why were social services on the case? I hadn't ever wanted to get them involved, all I wanted was for someone to help me sort John out, to sit him down and get him to admit his behaviour wasn't acceptable, to see the error of his ways and then we could get on with our lives. Normal, happy family lives. Was that too much to ask?

He'd been arrested, which I knew had to happen and it was part of the process, and he'd spent the night in a cell – the police will tell you that a night in a cell without the comforts of home often makes a person realise they have been an idiot and it's a wake-up call. That was how I saw this taking shape. How stupid was I?

John contacted his expensive solicitor and, after a chat with him, he was released to his mother's house (I wonder what she thought of it all) pending the court case. I was granted a Non-Molestation order and an

Occupation order, which should guarantee that the children and I could live at the house in safety, because any breach of these orders would mean serious repercussions for John.

A letter arrived on the doormat a few days later. It was from the Childcare Access Duty Social Worker of the local social services department, addressed to John and with a copy to me, and it read:

I am writing to inform you of our involvement regarding your children Alice and David. We have received two reports from the Police of domestic violence between yourself and your Wife. They state that there have been at least two assaults during which you have injured your Wife and they feel that many more may have gone unreported. They also state that your children are often present and that they feel that your children are suffering as a result.

The consequences for children living in a household where domestic violence occurs are well documented. They include risks to physical safety (of being used as a shield and being accidentally caught in the crossfire), poor role modelling of appropriate behaviour, responses to anger and supportive relationships and emotional harm from living in an atmosphere of tension, control and fear. These effects can have far reaching and long term implications for the children involved.

And it ended with the warning that if any further incidents were to occur, they would need to intervene and *'pursue this matter further'*.

I was horrified. Seeing this in writing from social

services came as a shock, in all honesty. All I wanted was for my husband to behave like a normal husband and father, and for us all to have a happy life together. I had made a cry for help, that's all. How could this be happening? We weren't the type of people who got involved with child protection agencies, for goodness' sake. John was a respected businessman, and I was a qualified nurse! I felt my circumstances were now the property of some faceless government organisation and it was a frightening thought.

I needed to get social services to let this go, or who knows where this might end? I was a good parent, and John was a good parent when he wanted to be – surely we didn't need this kind of intervention? Because my children were so young at the time, the idea of John's behaviour, the domestic violence, the shouting and bullying – all of it – actually having a tangible *and long-term* effect on them had not really occurred to me. Seeing it put in plain words in an official document made me realise, in an instant, that this was about far more than me wanting John to see sense and act like a well adjusted human being. This was about the safety, the health, the mental health and the well-being of my children. And not just now, while it was all going on, but *"these effects can have far reaching and long term implications for the children involved"*. Those words burned into my brain, or so it felt.

I was so ashamed, I couldn't tell a single soul.

The next thing that happened was, John's solicitor sent me his Defence Statement. Reading it threw me into a state of shock, a strange sense of reality having somehow been warped beyond recognition and I was the only one who spoke the truth. It was a horrific read. John took absolutely no responsibility at all for his behaviour, his moods, his anger – nothing. He showed no remorse, quite the opposite, in fact. He turned everything round to make it appear that *I was the one with the problems!*

The opening paragraph blamed me entirely, because of my *"behavioural tantrums"* which he said were *"largely associated with difficulties and problems"* that I had with my family. He described me as possessing *"a rather bad temper"* and said I would *"often fly into mad rages"*. So, basically, he was transferring his entire character and failings on to me – his victim! The letter went on…

It is accepted that there have been at least 3 to 4 occasions over recent months when there have been incidents of violence. The truth is that the Applicant cannot control her temper and whenever she flies into a rage, she is uncontrollable and she has punched and kicked me while screaming obscenities at me. My wife has a tendency to scream and hurl verbal abuse when she is in one of her mad furies. When she goes into this uncontrollable state, she cannot rationalise and will not listen to reason. When she behaves this way, in an attempt to protect myself and to prevent further attack, I have to restrain her by holding her arms. If you refer to the photographic evidence in the Applicants statement labelled 'PW1' the bruises shown are from when I have had to grab her to restrain her from using further violence against me.

And some of the statements left me literally speechless…

My wife bruises very easily.

I do not accept that I am capable of being a violent man.

My wife's statement portrays me as an extremely violent and dangerous man and this is certainly not the case. Her statement is wildly exaggerated and in most part it is untrue.

The denial and John's complete attack on me carried on, commenting on my recent diagnosis of anxiety. Yes, I was suffering with anxiety – because of the domestic violence and abuse, but John's statement used the information to claim that this made *me* more violent!

After an outpouring of blame, criticism, defamation and all manner of insults, John went on to say he had no desire to end the marriage! Adding insult to injury, as was his way, he stated that he believed I had *"no desire to separate or divorce"* but that my actions in applying for the Non-Molestation order and the Occupation order were *"to teach me a lesson"*.

The most laughable (but not in a good way) part of this whole barrage of lies was at the very end, where he had to sign to confirm that his statement was *"true to the best of my knowledge"*.

He was trying to make me appear as the bad guy, the source of all the domestic upheaval, and completely stark staring mad. Everything he was guilty of, he turned round on to me. It was his word against mine.

But, with the court orders in place, at least the house was peaceful and I felt safe. Even the children made comments about how much better things were for a while, although, being so young, they were soon missing their daddy and that started to get to me. I was, if you like, denying my son and daughter the right to have their father in their lives. That didn't make me feel good at all, whatever had happened before. They were missing the good side of John, the daddy who was silly and sweet, who entertained them and gave them exciting adventures that most children of their years wouldn't be ready for. He was fearless and he expected them to be, I think. They would go water skiing, snow-boarding – he'd even taken them on some mountain treks and they loved every minute of it all. He never cared what anyone else thought, he just got on with it, no matter what. Always a law unto himself. His way or no way, every time.

I wasn't enjoying life on my own. I wondered if this was how it would be, the single parent experience. The house was so quiet at times, I would turn the radio or the TV up loud, but that didn't help. And at bedtime, Alice and David would ask me every night, when could they see their daddy. It really hurt me that I was keeping them from him. And, in the end, I relented. John always told me I was weak. He was right.

He soon got in touch, possibly realising that I would perhaps have 'softened' and that, by now, I would be thinking that the children should see him. He seemed desperate to spend time with them and wanted to take them out somewhere for another adventure.

When they came back, we chatted. Stupidly, I'd had a couple of glasses of wine. Dutch courage. We both had a drink while we talked and the inevitable happened – we ended up in bed together. John was his charming, kind self again, telling me things I wanted to hear. And, of course, the children were absolutely delighted to find Daddy there the next morning.

And so, we returned to 'normal' and then the court case came around. John went in front of the judge, looking very handsome in his smart suit. The judge said it appeared that John had been quite violent towards me, and John, his head bowed in apparent acceptance and contrition, apologised. He explained that he'd been having business problems and also that he hadn't yet recovered from his father's death. He looked so forlorn, I felt really sorry for him. When John said he would seek counselling for his anger, and we would both attend for marriage guidance from the experts, I agreed to drop the charges and the judge dismissed the case, wishing us the best of luck.

On the way out of court, John turned to me and said, "See how easy it is to get away with something? It's all about how you play it." It was all a game to him and he'd got away with everything. And I had allowed that.

I was glad that social services were now out of the picture, and I told myself I had learned a valuable lesson. Never ask for help, because that would mean losing the children, or maybe being placed in a refuge with all the other abused women. I swore to myself that, from now on, I'd keep my head above the water, and I'd do it my way.

Chapter 17: The Not-so-Great Escape

Relate. I don't think anyone could have come up with a more fitting name for the service these people provide. The meaning of the word covers both *telling your story* and *forming a sympathetic relationship with another being*, so surely 'relate' was just what we, as a couple, needed. You'd think so.

But, instead of working *with* the counsellor, John couldn't help being himself. He refused to listen, he kept talking over her and would butt in constantly. It was so frustrating because the poor woman wasn't able to finish any of the points she was trying to make; he simply never let her speak. I kept apologising and telling John to be quiet and listen to her, but, as always, he was in his own world where only John knew all the answers, only John mattered.

"She's mad," he kept insisting in a loud voice while the counsellor was talking. "She's not normal, round the bloody twist because she wasn't brought up properly."

After only a few sessions, all following the same embarrassing pattern, the counsellor said she wasn't prepared to continue trying to get through to John, as she could see that communicating with him was impossible.

"I can only recommend that you two separate and seek a divorce. I can't see your situation changing because you" – she looked John straight in the eye – "you are not open to listening to anyone."

He was furious at her because she wouldn't agree with him that I was a mad woman and everything was my fault.

"Can't you see my wife's abnormal – damaged? Anybody can see that!"

John seemed almost shocked that someone didn't agree with him, wouldn't give credence to his claims that I was useless, stupid, a waste of space. It was humiliating, but I could see that this professional lady had worked out for herself quite early on, just what the scenario was.

Something many people don't understand, because they haven't had any connection with domestic abuse or being controlled by a partner, is that constant, on-going, relentless mental and physical abuse actually changes the way your mind works. It changes the way you perceive things, the way you think and process information. It changes who you are.

When I look back, I can see how this actually played out in my own situation, and it makes me realise how easily some people can come close to being destroyed by staying with a controlling partner. All it takes is for two very different types of individual to come together in a relationship, one person who is patient, tolerant and forgiving, and the other who is manipulative, self-absorbed and driven to control their partner. The first person would be described by others as warm and friendly, the second as cold and distant, and so on.

John's ceaseless controlling behaviour, supported totally by his mother and sister, started to wear me down and it was no longer enough that I didn't fight back, didn't say or do anything to upset or provoke: nothing on earth would put an end to the cruelty.

Although, in my own mind, I know that I wasn't any of those awful things John would call me, eventually I reached a place where I began to doubt myself, to question if he might actually be right. My self-esteem had been chipped away to almost zero, my confidence likewise, and I could feel something quite sinister taking over.

It's now a long time since the last of the physical bruises healed, but I've learned that the mental-emotional 'bruising' never really gets better. That relentless drip, drip, drip of insults, slurs on my character, the ridicule heaped on my family, the threats to my personal safety and the safety of my children – all of it, had left permanent scars. Even now, certain things can hurl my mind back in an instant, to the tension, the panic and the fear.

One of the words John would use frequently to

belittle me was 'thick'.

"You're so thick! You're stupid! Your family are all thick religious nutters!"

Even now, years later, I can be shopping in a supermarket or the local grocery shop, when I'll spot a label on some ordinary, mundane item, such as custard, soup or yoghurt, where the product is proudly described as 'extra thick' and it's as if someone punches me in the head. A split-second wave of nausea flashes through me, making me gasp for breath, then I look away and fight back the tears. And, no matter how many times I remind myself that now it's all behind me, it still keeps happening. The damage does not go away.

I started to have panic attacks while I was driving, I began to suffer with migraines, and my blood pressure was up. All because of living with John. But it hadn't only affected me, I soon realised.

Alice was six years old by this time and I could see little habits developing that made me realise she had been damaged, too. Her dad was always slamming doors. In fact, he seemed incapable of closing a door properly. Unfortunately, Alice had the room directly above the lounge, and that was where most of John's outbursts and the verbal abuse would take place. No matter how I would beg him to keep his voice down when he was yelling at me about what a 'piece of filth' I was, because the children would hear and they'd be upset, he wouldn't listen, so Alice must have heard a lot of what went on. John would say it didn't matter because "she already knows what a piece of filth you are, anyway."

The hardest part of all of this for me is to have realised that it wasn't just myself being harmed, but my two little innocent children were being affected in very bad ways by what they were witnessing. In terms of what constitutes abuse, forcing or allowing children to witness domestic violence or any other form of abuse, is, in itself, child abuse.

Alice's anger was being played out in this door slamming and she was doing it with such force that the door frames were cracking. She also became fearful of some quite normal everyday things and situations, such as seeing a flock of birds flying overhead, or finding a drawer not quite fully closed. She would start crying and curl up in a ball, inconsolable. She was suffering from acute anxiety.

Yes, it broke my heart. Of course it did. So, why didn't I now find the strength to leave? Because John's control had become more frightening, more evil, than ever before.

I was already aware that John knew some rather strange characters. When he had a problem with a client who was taking too long to pay or whatever, and John ran out of patience, he would organise a 'debt collector' and then the money would suddenly materialise. He would tell me sometimes that he knew people who could 'make somebody disappear' and I knew he told me that for a reason. It was a threat, not even a veiled one, and it was the ultimate in control: he was telling me that if I tried to leave him, he would have me harmed, or perhaps even killed.

He used to tell me if I ever really left him, he would arrange a 'little accident' – and not just for me, but for my family as well.

So, I lived in a state of constant fear and dread – would I perhaps accidentally annoy him one day, and find myself face to face with one of his thugs? I can't describe how it felt to try so very hard to pretend that everything was fine, to get on with life as a wife and mother (which is all I wanted), and to see my little girl showing signs that she really wasn't coping with the things she witnessed. Why should she? She was a child.

David, on the other hand, seemed to be free from any ill effects because he was closely involved with his dad, and they would go off together to enjoy all of the exciting activities John would dream up. I suppose, because David always went along with these plans and ideas, John had no reason to be annoyed with him. In fact, John must have felt that David was on his side. But I always wondered if our son was just trying to help keep the peace, and maybe he wasn't happy doing it. He never said.

Alice became incredibly picky with her meals and would only eat a very limited range of foods. I knew she wasn't getting enough nutrients and she was losing weight. This was a cause for great concern to me and I tried to get her to talk whenever we were on our own. But she wouldn't open up and I didn't want to push her.

Then came the dreadful news about the Twin

Towers in New York. You couldn't look in any direction without seeing a TV screen or a newspaper with those terrible images of planes crashing into the tall buildings, and hearing the reports of how many people had lost their lives, how many were missing... it was shocking and terribly sad. I'm sure the months and months of reporting around the world would have affected a lot of people and resulted in a real fear of flying. Alice's anxiety was worse after this.

I took her to see our GP but I couldn't, didn't dare, mention what was going on at home, in fear of the possible reprisals. I could *not* risk social services getting involved again. The doctor did blood tests and it came to light that the restricted diet was causing health issues. I was instructed to put Alice on special foods straight away.

John was growing increasingly cruel towards me, as if he was supremely confident that he could get away with anything at all. Whenever his pinching, slapping or hitting caused me to bruise, I would try to hide the marks from the children, but sometimes they'd notice and that made me feel utterly ashamed.

After a particularly shocking incident that ended with him throwing his full dinner plate at the wall and the food spattering everywhere, all the while shouting and swearing, frightening the children, I told him he needed to leave the house.

"You fucking leave! It's my house, not yours! Don't give me that peasant food again – it's only fit for pigswill! My mother's disgusted with the meals you give me!"

The children and I left our food and took ourselves out of his way into the lounge, while John stomped off to his office down the hallway. I decided we must not stay at the house.

I wouldn't get the police involved because of what that would inevitably lead to. Telling David and Alice to be quiet and stay there, I sneaked upstairs and quickly packed a bag for the three of us. I was determined to leave this time. Hurrying the children into the car and stuffing the bag in the boot, I got into the driver's seat just as John appeared at the door. He picked up a large plant pot and threw it towards the car. It smashed on the driveway and broke into pieces, sending soil and bits of plant everywhere. This was closely followed by several others, so I got us out of there pretty quickly.

David kept asking, "What's Daddy doing? What have we done wrong?"

I tried to calm them both. "Daddy's not well just now. He needs help so he can get better."

They were both so upset and all I could think was how unfair all of this was on two children who had done nothing to deserve any of it.

I drove to a small, inexpensive hotel and booked us in, still shaking but trying to reassure David and Alice, who weren't at all happy with being taken to this place that was nothing like home – very far from it! But this was all I could afford right now.

I kept the children off school the next day, as I couldn't handle them telling anyone what was happening in our family life. But I didn't have enough money or toys and books with me to keep them entertained, especially in a strange place that didn't feel at all homely. The day passed rather uncomfortably for all of us.

Every now and then I'd think maybe I should contact the police, but the thought of social services getting involved again, with the outcome that I didn't dare even guess at, was enough to stop me. Too risky.

David was nagging me to go back home. "I want to play my computer games – there's nothing to do here. Please can we go home?" Alice was sad and anxious. This wasn't a good situation for either of them. I had convinced them we needed to stay away until their dad calmed down, but I couldn't keep that going for very long. I also didn't have much cash on me. I felt trapped.

We went back to the house around midday. The driveway was still the same mess, littered with broken plant pots and soil, and now dead plants. The first thing to enter my head was to wonder what on earth the postman must have thought. Once again, worrying about what other people would think.

John would have known I couldn't stay away for long without cash or sufficient clothes and so on, but he had decided he'd get a solicitor's letter to me anyway – it was waiting for me on the hallway table. His solicitor did anything John told him to, and the letter was disgusting. As always, he was throwing everything on to me, claiming I was the one with problems, the one who needed help.

'Your husband claims you became violent in front of the children... your behaviour was out of control... our client suggests that you seek professional help... we must advise you not to take the children away from the family home again...'

I was appalled. John was making me out to be the mad one and he knew I couldn't even afford to get a solicitor to write a reply. It was all so very wrong and, yet again, here I was, back where he wanted me. I felt useless, paralysed.

A neighbour saw me clearing up the debris and came over. "I hear you had a break-in, Paula. I'm so sorry. Are you OK?"

"It wasn't a break-in, Jenny, it's because John upset one of his clients. It's shocking what people will do."

"Well, John's obviously not very well liked, is he?" As she spoke, I thought I saw a look of pity in her eyes.

John came home that evening and he knew we'd be there. He offered no apology, nothing. He just carried on as if everything was back to normal.

"Hi, kids! You OK? Did Mum take you somewhere new? Silly Mum!"

Chapter 18: Impossible to Explain

My situation was almost surreal. I was a mental and emotional yo-yo, being flung back and forth between two extreme scenarios. One, where my brain kept telling me I needed to leave, to get myself and the children the hell away from this madman and his evil control, whatever it took.

And two, where my overwhelming emotions told me the children needed their parents, their family, to be whole and not fractured, and that breaking everything apart could only cause them pain and problems. By far the worst aspect of all, was my persevering faith in our marriage, in my husband when he was being his good self, and in my determination that one day he would – what? – wake up and realise how happy he could be if he just stopped turning into that violent, out-of-control, abusive character that he so easily became?

I asked myself a million times, what was it that made him switch from one to the other, so quickly and without any apparent trigger? The only answer I could ever come up with was that I must be the one causing him to change, that it had to be something I was doing, or not doing, or maybe just something in *me*, the person I was. And that made me feel partly responsible.

John's constant digs and insults over time had definitely taken their toll and made me doubt myself, and that doubt had become very real to me. My self-esteem had all but disappeared, I had little or no confidence, my nerves were on edge all the time and I couldn't relax. I felt worthless and incredibly weakened under John's forceful and unrelenting control. It was as if he had been chipping away at every aspect of the person I had been, my beliefs, my ideals – everything – and now there was very little of me left.

And this is exactly how people like John perform. They don't seem to want or need the kind of loving, harmonious relationships most of us work towards: what they crave is to control, and once that control is firmly in place, then they abuse.

Those of us who don't suffer from any personality disorder, or whatever the professionals call the aberration that causes some people to deviate so far from what most of us regard as 'normal' behaviour, unless we are mental health experts, cannot understand it, can't deal with it, and – take it from me – can't change it.

Although by now I was far from the hopeful, determined being John had met on that fateful evening years ago, I was still hanging on to some semblance of sanity, although I thank my children for that because I'm certain I would have given up, had it not been for them.

And so I began to do some homework, to find out what John's problem could be. What sort of condition could he have that turned him into a monster in the blink of an eye? If I could find out, surely that would be a step in the right direction?

I researched psychopathy. Mental health professionals do warn us laymen and women to be very careful when looking into such specific personality conditions, especially when it comes to the checklist of the characteristics that, when all boxes are ticked, can assist in the diagnosis of a psychopath.

My eyes ran down the list, again and again. The traits that could suggest a psychopathic personality include: a lack of remorse, lack of empathy and a callous nature. When had I ever seen John show remorse for any of the awful things he'd done? Not once. And I decided long ago that empathy was not something he was familiar with. And callous? Yes, most definitely. Then there's a disregard for the law and social norms; refusal to accept any responsibility for his actions. All boxes ticked so far. A need for stimulation: he could never sit still for long, he always had to be up and doing something and it was normally something daring or dangerous, the adrenalin buzz. Then I read 'egocentric personality' and I reminded myself of how John had never been the slightest bit interested in my past life or my family, and how all of his conversation was about himself, his business, his success, his family.

Apparently, a psychopath will use charm or

violence to get his or her own way. Tick on both counts. This wasn't making me feel any better, and no matter how many times I told myself there must be a lot of people who meet some of these criteria, I couldn't ignore the feeling that I'd just had my worst fears confirmed. I knew these tests could only be used properly by the professionals, but it didn't change how I felt now.

So, was John to be feared – or pitied? I do think I felt both, possibly in equal measure. I have always had empathy for my fellow human beings, and I couldn't imagine for a second what it would be like to be totally incapable of having such feelings. As for not giving a hoot about the law, never feeling remorse, having to constantly experience things that give you a 'rush' and never being able to just stop and smell the roses, so to speak... it's almost as if these people are not quite human.

Even if John wasn't a true psychopath, these specific traits are signs of personality disorder of some kind; I realised that I'd known for a long time that he did have something wrong with him and it was illustrated very clearly in the way he dealt with people and situations.

This gave me yet another dilemma. It was a sort of relief to have my suspicions confirmed about John's state of mind, but, at the same time, how was I supposed to deal with him now, knowing he really needed professional help?

Being completely honest, a part of me felt truly

sorry for him. He was the father of my amazing children and he obviously couldn't cope with normal, everyday life. He found it impossible to control his 'other self', even in public when I could see people looking at him as he shouted and swore loudly about what 'scum' I was, what a 'mad woman' he'd married, and how my family were 'all filth, the lot of them!' I knew he was the one they were all thinking was the mad one, not me.

I couldn't help but feel some empathy for this man who, when in his right mind, was a funny, playful and interesting father and an attentive, loving husband, but then his other personality would take over, and he'd become the man who seemed to have no control over his own actions. It was pitiful.

I am aware that those who have had no personal experience of a violent, controlling partner could so easily see me as some weak, pathetic woman who 'keeps going back for more' and so probably 'gets what she deserves'. I do get that. It's only when you live through this yourself that you comprehend the conflict of thoughts and emotions that pull you back and then push you away, again and again, and how the never-ending mental-emotional struggle to do the right thing – and not just for yourself, but for everyone concerned – wears you down so that you start to lose your grip on the reality of your own situation.

Within a matter of days, I would be dragged from my beliefs that 'he really does love me and the children, he's making quite an effort now, the children are so happy with him, it's all going to be fine' to the equally strong realisation that 'he's never going to change, I'm going to have to leave, he's definitely got something wrong with him, I'm terrified of him'. And I felt an equal pull from both.

Chapter 19: Holding On

From past experience, I knew all too well that I needed to build up some level of independence, especially financially, so that I wouldn't be so completely reliant on John. The money side of things was a huge part of his control, and if I could just get some cash behind me, I knew I'd feel I was in a stronger position. It would be a start.

I often helped out at the local primary school that David and Alice attended, and that had led to them offering me an official position as a teaching assistant. I accepted, most gratefully, and enjoyed spending time working with the children. This went well for a while and John was in one of his good phases, but after a few weeks he started being nasty to me, especially in the mornings when I was looking forward to my little job.

He would hurl insults at me about how thick I was, how the school would soon realise I was totally incompetent and I'd be sacked. He would shove me into the kitchen units or punch my arm for absolutely no reason as he pushed past me, knowing I would be bruised. His anger would escalate day after day and, once it reached fever pitch, I would be so upset and in pain from the injuries, I couldn't possibly go in to work. How could I have put on a big smile and walked into that classroom of little girls and boys, pretending to be happy and full of fun? I couldn't, I was too demoralised after these extreme bullying sessions.

And I couldn't tell anyone what was going on. I was so ashamed. Whenever I had to have contact with anyone – in a shop, for instance, or when the postman came – I was acutely aware that, under the clothes I was wearing, I was covered in bruises and swollen flesh, and that my life was the same, damage hidden beneath a façade of normality.

I knew John's outbursts at this time were the result of his anger and frustration at my attempt to 'do my own thing' because to him it meant he was losing some of the control he had over me.

He wasn't going to allow me to carry on with my nice little job, and if I persisted in trying to hang on to it, I was only making things much worse for myself. So, when John decided I should go back to working for him again, I agreed. There was no point in arguing, and if it meant putting a stop to the bullying and the beatings, then so be it. According to him, I'd never left the business anyway – an illustration of his absolute denial of anything he didn't control.

This wasn't as bad as it had been first time around, due to the company having grown and expanded to a point where there was plenty of work for me to do without having to be located in his office. I could still work part-time and do everything at home. At least this way I could be left alone and not have to deal with people, not have to lie and pretend.

There was a catch. Of course there was. Instead of paying me actual money, John said I could have a credit card to use for whatever I wanted – clothes, hairdressers, toiletries, gifts and so on. It was in joint names, so he could monitor what I spent, what I bought, and, more to the point, he could track my movements according to the places and dates on all receipts. More control.

John explained the conditions of me having this card. Under no circumstances was I to attempt to draw cash, to pay for a solicitor's services or for hotel bills.

I got on with the work, took care of the children and the home, and John went off each day to his cherished company. We stumbled along like this for quite some time: as long as I played by his rules, life was at least bearable. And, as always, whenever things improved, I would hope against hope that this was it, that we'd reached a turning-point, and so on.

My relationship with my family was, on the surface, non-existent, but in total secret I would meet Dad and Shirley for a coffee and a chat. John was never a part of our conversation.

There was an unfortunate incident once, when I found myself desperate for someone to have the children for a few hours – I think I had a medical appointment that I'd almost forgotten until the last minute – which was very unusual because they were normally always with me if they weren't at school. I rang Dad and he very kindly said straight away that he and Shirley would be happy to have them for the day.

When I rang Dad to say I was ready to pick them up, he asked if they could pop David and Alice back to me, but only if I could assure him that John wouldn't be there. It shouldn't have been a problem if John had stuck to his normally predictable routine, but, as luck would have it, he turned up while they were still with me in the garden. I'd been showing them around the place, pointing out the various improvements we'd made to the property, because it had been years since they'd visited – since none of my family had been able to come near for a long while. It was as if I felt I needed to demonstrate something good and positive about my life with John.

Worst of all, the children were saying cheerio to their grandparents and they were all hugging each other by Dad's car, when I heard John's car coming up the road. I held my breath and my heart was pounding. I knew what was about to happen.

John leapt out of his car as if it was on fire, slammed the door and started shouting and swearing at the top of his voice, waving his arms around like someone possessed.

"You filthy peasants! What are you doing at my house?"

Then he swung round to glare at Shirley and almost screamed at her, "Look at you! You fat filthy pig!"

As he strode towards the house, he shouted over his shoulder, "Get out of here! Fuck off, you filthy cunts! Take your fucking fat pig with you and don't come back!" The tirade of abuse carried on, even when Dad's car was well out of sight.

I was gutted. The children had witnessed John's appalling behaviour, they'd seen how their father could lose all control and attack their loving grandparents with the worst verbal abuse imaginable. Their little faces spoke volumes.

John's worst outbursts were always followed immediately by a complete switch to him being the best dad in the world, and the children would (apparently, and so I believed) forget what had happened and they'd be happy and delighted with whatever he came up with next, whether that was a holiday or an adventure, or, as on one such occasion, he bought a boat. What I couldn't possibly have known at the time was that everything John was splashing the money on was all through finance arrangements.

The children had inherited from both of us a love of boats and the water, and they could scarcely contain themselves when he showed them the gleaming white 30-foot family cruiser.

John arranged a permanent mooring at Great Yarmouth on the Norfolk coast and we'd drive out for a weekend on the ocean wave whenever he decided he could leave the business for long enough. I thought that being out on the boat for a while, with all that fresh air and a nice calm sea, would mean John was totally occupied and having fun with the children, who absolutely loved the experience.

But, even then, as soon as he had an audience of any kind – the people on their boat in the next mooring or passers-by on the quayside – he'd start shouting his insults and obscenities, all aimed at me but meant for everyone in the vicinity to hear.

"Look at my stupid wife! She's a thick bastard! She wasn't brought up properly!"

It was appalling and I was completely humiliated, to the point of huddling down as low as I could get beside the cabin, to avoid the pitying glances from total strangers. I could never reason with John that this was unacceptable behaviour and he'd just tell me I was paranoid, too bothered about what other folk thought, and that I couldn't take criticism. How could he not understand that everyone saw him as a disgusting person who was humiliating his wife in public with his dreadful verbal abuse?

"Look at your mum, kids! She's paranoid! She thinks everyone's looking at her!"

No matter what I said, he would turn it around to be my fault, my problem.

Dad and Shirley didn't get in touch at all after that last awful, unforgivable episode, and I wondered if they thought they should leave me to deal with my own mess, because it was impossible for them to get involved.

I did start to consider that the life I found myself

living was the result of my own actions. I should have married a good Christian man, a man with strong beliefs and ethics, not this man who showed compassion for no-one, not even his own wife and children.

Another thing I repeatedly thought about was the existence of evil in some people. I had been taught that there was both good and evil in the world, and I was always really shocked at the way John reacted to any mention of church or any connection with Christianity.

If I let myself follow that line of thought, I would tell myself that John had something evil about him. Whenever we drove past a church, he would always shout out of the open car window, "Fucking Jesus Christ! Fucking religious bastards!", even when there was no-one there, just a little stone church with its bell tower and stained glass windows.

We weren't allowed to attend church, not even at Christmas for the carol service, and – believe it or not – I wasn't allowed to walk along the pavement on the same side of the road as the church!

How utterly absurd.

Chapter 20: On the Inside, Looking In

I know that much of what I felt at the time was shame, and, having been raised to believe that I should never be, say or do anything to bring shame on myself, my family or anyone else, the only way I could deal with this was to pretend it wasn't really there.

I was already ashamed that my first marriage hadn't worked out, even though I wasn't the one to go off with someone else, and I was the one left in pieces. The shame was that, for whatever reason, I had not been able to make my marriage a success (it always hurt that I never knew why), and then I became a divorced woman, bringing even more shame.

The dreadful guilt I carried for giving in to John's demands over the abortion was a burden I would bear for the rest of my life.

And so, finding myself now a battered wife, totally dependent on my abusive husband and completely trapped in this cycle of the domestic violence storms punctuated by periods of calm and hope, I was so utterly ashamed I couldn't speak of it to anyone. I even pretended *to myself* that things weren't as bad as they really were.

Like so many other people who live as a victim of their partner, I somehow reached a point where I felt sorry for John. Sorry because of what must be happening in his mind, in order to make him behave that way towards the people he should cherish, protect and love. I couldn't imagine what it must take to drive someone to lash out like he did, and with no provocation that anyone could detect. It had to be mental illness, surely – there couldn't be any other explanation.

I knew John's mother would never consider such an idea, so he would get no support from her, and his sister was so deeply entrenched with the mother that she wouldn't dream of speaking against either of them, even if she knew or suspected that John was troubled in his mind. I did often think she knew more than she appeared to.

It was clear to me that he had nobody in his life who would help him and it was equally clear that he did need proper, professional help, but I knew there was no way he would ever entertain that idea, not in a million years. As his wife and, apparently, the only person to see John as he really was, this tormented soul, I felt I needed to keep trying to help 'good John' to completely take over 'bad John'. And the only way this could be achieved, I believed with all of my heart, was to continue to be there, to show him in every possible way that the children and I were there for him, that we loved him and cared about him.

Now, I realise that my thinking was so skewed by the on-going abuse and the stress, but – just like John – I was on my own in this mess and had no-one to guide me, to help me.

My good friend, Kate, who never gave up on me and to whom I will be eternally grateful, would keep in touch from time to time, just to check that I was alright. She knew when it was OK to contact me and we would chat on the phone or sometimes we'd meet for coffee in town when I was shopping. I knew I could trust her implicitly and I started to open up a bit and tell her some of what was going on. I wasn't at all surprised when she told me she'd known for quite a while that I was struggling and that everything in my garden was far from rosy. She didn't try to persuade me to do anything, she didn't offer advice or try to influence me in any way, but she did say she knew a counsellor who I could speak to.

"She's been through quite a lot herself and she talks sense, not gobbledegook. It would be in strict confidence, just between you and her, and it might do you some good – anyway, what have you got to lose?"

I made an appointment and went along to meet this woman with very mixed feelings. I was fearful, worried that John would know where I was, even though I'd prepared a good cover story in case he questioned me; I was slightly hopeful that she might, by some miracle, be able to help; and I was partly resigned to my increasingly overriding belief that nobody in the world could do anything for me.

Her name was Helen. She didn't ask me any questions, which at first I thought was odd. She spoke calmly and with a warmth that made me feel quite relaxed, for the first time in ages. While I sipped my fruit tea, she told me her own story that had led to her eventually becoming a counsellor. Even hearing only the nutshell version, I was struck by the similarities with my own situation, and it was strangely reassuring to finally realise *I wasn't the only one!*

"Have you ever heard of Stockholm Syndrome?" she asked me and I shook my head.

"The term originated when four people were taken hostage by bank robbers in Stockholm, Sweden, and held against their will in the bank vault for six days together with their captors, and then set free. What was astonishing was that the released hostages felt a strong empathy for their captors and they refused to give evidence against them in court! The public were up in arms, completely shocked by this apparent lack of any desire on the part of the hostages to see the culprits brought to justice.

"It transpired that, during their enforced imprisonment, the robbers had talked openly and at length with the hostages about why they were committing the crime, about their lives and their families and so on, and through this a strong bond had formed between the two groups, with the hostages feeling empathy for their captors and not carrying any animosity towards them for what they had done."

Hearing this from someone who understood the psychology of the situation did help to explain a lot of what I was feeling. The trouble was, it served to reinforce my idea that I needed to help John, and did nothing to strengthen my resolve to leave him.

Chapter 21: A Bridge Too Far

Life carried on in its unpredictable fashion, but I would always make the most of the better times, especially when it meant the children could enjoy playing with their friends and being carefree. Watching them doing normal family things gave me a great deal of pleasure – and it gave me hope, too.

Although as a couple we didn't have what you'd call close friends, there were a number of long-standing acquaintances and local people who we knew quite well, and in the summer months we would often have a barbecue and invite everyone. These people were all familiar with John's little quirks, as they put it, but they had never seen his other side, so when he blatantly walked past guests whose drinks glasses were empty, or when he suddenly switched off the music because he didn't like that particular song, they found the whole thing amusing.

John was lacking in any ability to do things around the house and garden, and he had never even tried to learn to cook anything. If ever, on a very rare occasion, he did attempt to do something, it would go wrong and that was it – he would flip. I couldn't help but find it exasperating to see him struggling with the food on the barbecue and having no clue whatsoever as to which bits of meat were cooked and which were still raw! I never said anything, but would just take over the cooking duties as well as fetching drinks and laying out all the food – it really was like having a third child sometimes.

The trouble with social events was, I could choose times for most of them to suit John's moods, but when it came to birthdays I had no choice. I did everything I could to make birthdays special, because that's how it had been for me as a child.

Alice's ninth birthday was coming round and she had asked if she could have a stretch limousine to take her and her friends for a drive around and then to a pizza restaurant out of town. It was all arranged and booked, but on the day John's mood took a turn for the worse: it seemed there would always be something to tip the scale, and he'd already been moaning about the cost of the birthday party. As usual, my family were the match that lit the blue touch-paper.

John's mother had given Alice a hundred pounds and then he spotted the card my dad had sent, with a cheque for ten pounds inside. That was it, he couldn't control his anger.

"Bloody mean bastards! A tenner? Is that it? My mother gave Alice a hundred – that's a proper present! Tight religious bastards!"

I hoped John would stay away from the party because now I knew his mood was only going to get worse. He kept muttering obscenities about my family under his breath and a feeling of dread started to creep over me.

Surprisingly, he made it through most of the day, but I could tell his temper was brewing. The limo pulled up at the restaurant entrance and a babble of happy girls and boys piled out and giggled their way inside. John was still outside somewhere and, when I looked around to see where he was, I saw him striding up and down, shouting at passers-by.

"I married a mad woman! Her family are all mad as well! Stupid religious bastards!" and so on.

I could see the faces of the people walking by, and they were obviously thinking he was either drunk or on drugs and they were giving him a wide berth, then they'd look back at him and comment to each other. All I could do was watch from the restaurant window and hope he wouldn't come in to spoil Alice's fun. I could hear a couple of people in the restaurant talking about the mad man outside.

Luckily, some of the children's parents arrived early to take them home and a couple of them asked me why John was strutting up and down the pavement, apparently so deep in thought. What could I say? I just shrugged my shoulders. All I wanted now was to get back home safely, preferably without incident.

John drove his car round to pick us up and I wasn't keen to get in with him in his pent-up state, but I had

Alice, David and one of David's pals with me, so I had no choice. I got the children fastened in the back seats and was halfway into the front passenger seat when, all of a sudden, the car lurched forward and in seconds we were doing sixty miles an hour – in the car park.

Then, without warning, John stood on the brake pedal and I shot forward into the windscreen, my head bashing against it. I have no idea how the glass didn't break with the impact, and my head hurt like hell. I quickly fastened my seat belt.

We drove home in silence, John not even acknowledging the incident. The kids ran into the house with their gifts and I went to get the birthday cake out of the boot. As I was leaning in, something smashed on my head incredibly hard. It was John. He had come up behind me and banged his fist down as hard as he could on the very top of my head. A wave of nausea and shock ran through me, and the pain in my head was now indescribable. Then I realised I could feel bits of teeth in my mouth. John stormed into the house, shouting at me as he went.

"That's what you deserved today! Useless woman! Who the hell could put up with you?"

I was sobbing now and had to get upstairs as quickly as I could to avoid the children seeing the state I was in. Looking in the mirror, I opened my mouth and spat broken bits of tooth into the hand basin. I looked dreadful and was feeling dizzy: I knew I needed to get medical help, so I booked a cab.

Heading into Casualty at the hospital, I thought

about telling them what had really happened, but that same fear of social services taking the children away took over again and I changed my mind. I told them I'd fallen downstairs.

One brain scan later, I was told to take painkillers and rest, then go to my dentist the following day. I got back to the house in the dead of night and John and the kids were all asleep. What a sad day it had been, and how I hated John.

My dentist took one look at me and I knew it was pointless saying I'd fallen downstairs. It had only been a year or so since he'd done quite a bit of work for me and I'd been so proud of my new straightened smile.

"Paula, I think I know what's caused this damage. Is there anything you'd like to talk about? In the strictest confidence, of course."

I felt so deflated, I couldn't even argue or try to deny the truth.

"My husband has bouts of severe depression and he can't cope. Things get on top of him..." It sounded weak.

"Well, then he needs to seek help – or perhaps you should think about what *you* need to do?"

"Yes, I know... please don't mention anything in my records – I can't bear for anyone to know."

He patted my hand and sighed. I got the feeling I wasn't the first woman to be sitting in his chair in this state. He did as much temporary work as he could, and made me an appointment for me to have crowns fitted and the work completed properly. It was an expensive episode, but I had my credit card.

As usual, there was no apology from John, no regret at what he'd done to me. The only thing he did say was, "You deserved it – your family were mean to Alice".

This extreme incident changed something for me. It was impossible to hide my damaged teeth and some of the other mothers at school asked me what on earth had happened. I lied, of course, but I was deluding myself if I thought they believed me for a second. From this point forward, I decided to keep my life private.

Chapter 22: Holiday in Hell

When you are the person *trapped inside* a destructive and abusive relationship, you cannot see the situation objectively and your decisions are based more on a desperate desire for normality, than on any balanced assessment. The problem is, you don't understand this while you remain *trapped inside*.

That last appalling incident had left me with more questions than ever. It was becoming all too clear that John did have mental health issues, but would he ever get over these, or would he become worse over time? Was there anything I could do to help him? What could I do to prevent him having the worst episodes? And so on. As the questions whirled around in my head, I had one overriding thought, and that was to somehow find a way to leave John – but without risking all of the scenarios he would threaten me with, the things I was desperate to avoid. The main threat was losing my children, or, much worse, seeing them left with their damaged father, and I had to do everything in my power to make sure that didn't happen.

Meanwhile, all I could do was play the good wife, look after the children and keep them safe, and placate John as much as possible to try and keep the peace. And, behind the scenes, I would start working on my Grand Plan, whatever that was going to be. I had no idea.

True to his pattern of behaviour, having just recently caused the worst incident so far, John announced that we were having a family holiday and that he'd booked us into a really swish hotel on Gran Canaria, for a whole two weeks.

Now that the children were getting older and more independent, I thought this holiday would be less demanding and so, hopefully, John could unwind and be more tolerant. Maybe, just maybe, he wouldn't have to go off every night like he'd always done before. I also knew that I would feel safe in a big hotel complex with lots of people around twenty-four hours a day.

We landed on the island to find our destination was beautiful and the weather perfect for a relaxing stay. The hotel was nothing short of fabulous, a huge palatial expanse of white-washed stone buildings surrounded by lush sub-tropical gardens, beyond which the golden sand dunes stretched in their graceful curves. Paradise. The Riu Palace Hotel in Meloneras.

Situated right by the sea with golden sandy beaches, the hotel had five fresh-water swimming pools and a children's pool, a promenade offering a wealth of seafood restaurants, shopping malls crammed with high-end boutiques, a solarium terrace and this gorgeous climate – who could fail to have a wonderful time in a place like this?

The first evening felt really special, like a normal family having a normal holiday. We talked and laughed together, chose our dishes from the menu together, enjoyed the Spanish music and then all went off to check out the entertainment, which proved to be spectacular. As I watched John so apparently at ease with the children, I almost wept. This was what I always knew we could be, and it felt so right, so good.

We were all ready for a night's sleep, so we went up to the family suite together. John poured us both a drink while Alice and David got ready for bed. As soon as I had them settled, John just got up and left. No word, nothing. The same as on previous holidays, off he went on his own and I was left to stay with the kids. I won't pretend I was fine with it but I wouldn't say anything, I just kept my disappointment to myself. I heard him come bumbling in at 3am.

The next morning, of course, the children tried to wake their dad so we could all go down for breakfast together. He wasn't going to budge and even started to get cross with them, so they gave up. I could see they were unhappy at his refusal to join us, and I could hear other families playing together outside in the sunshine. The three of us went down to the dining room and I tried to make light of it.

"Don't worry, Dad works very hard all the time so we should let him rest when he's on holiday. He can join us again later."

After eating a delicious breakfast, we ventured outside and found some sun loungers under a palm tree, so I settled down with my book while the youngsters investigated and played. I enjoyed the sun and the luxurious surroundings, and even managed to nod off for a while. It really was a beautiful place.

It was around lunchtime when John appeared, and the children were pleased to see him. They laughed at how he'd smothered too much sun cream over himself, telling him, "You're a snowman! You'll melt in the sun!" Then he lay on his lounger and before long his mobile started beeping. He would always receive business calls when we were away, and he would talk to these people for ages without even mentioning to them that he was on holiday with his family. He never switched off, just like his phone.

A bit later, he had a swim with the children and then went to sleep, to be awakened by the sound of a text coming through on my mobile. It was my brother, Michael, letting us know that his wife, Carol, had given birth to twins! How exciting! The babies had arrived earlier than expected and I had hoped to be back home for the birth. I sat up, excited at the news.

"How lovely, they've had twins! I'll call Michael now." I picked the phone up but John's angry voice stopped me.

"No! You're not calling those imbeciles! Bringing more filth into the world! More thick bastards to join your stupid religious family!"

People were turning to look in our direction

because, as usual, John was speaking so loudly. He was red in the face with anger. David told him to be quiet, but nobody could ever stop him, not even his own child.

"What's wrong with Dad?" Alice looked at me, her little face anxious, needing reassurance.

John was out of control now, boiling mad – all because of my brother's new babies. I stood up to leave. I wanted to get away from the humiliation and embarrassment. John carried on.

"See! You don't like the truth, do you?" he ranted. "Tell these people here what a family I married into!"

Some of those nearby were shaking their heads at him, but he never got it – they weren't disapproving of me, it was *him*.

"She doesn't like anyone staring at her, you know – she's paranoid! Go ahead and look! Take a good look at what I married!" He was getting louder and louder. "My wife is absolute filth!"

Alice and David followed me, but where would we go? This wonderful place of paradise was suddenly a prison and I had nowhere to run to. I asked at Reception if we could have an additional room, but they needed John's bank card for that. I thought I'd try the holiday rep, who we'd met when we arrived.

I found the young lady and told her I needed to get myself and my children home as quickly as possible because I was having problems with my husband, but she didn't take me seriously, telling me I should try and relax and enjoy the holiday! I had two weeks to get through and I had no idea how the children and I would manage it.

John walked into the room later and shouted at me, "I hope you're going to apologise to me! And to our children for how stubborn and awkward you are!"

In stark contrast to the previous evening, the children and I went down to the dining room together and I thought the other guests were looking at me, wondering where John was. That's how it felt, anyway. Sheer humiliation. David and Alice were very quiet through the meal, and I felt so sorry for them. They had had one day of a happy holiday with their mum and dad, and then disaster – and whatever the next two weeks were going to bring.

We saw John arrive in the dining room and sit at a table on his own. He appeared to be in his familiar 'trance' state and didn't seem to be aware of his surroundings, or that we were there. I began to dread the night that was fast approaching.

He didn't come back to the room at all, but went straight out after his dinner and came back in the early hours, making sure he disturbed us all. He opened the door on to the balcony and, to my horror, started talking loudly about what a loser I was and how I needed help with my mental problems, how I wasn't brought up properly... he wouldn't stop.

There was a knock at the door. It was the couple in the next suite asking if everything was OK. Now, John had an audience.

"Apart from my mad wife, I'm fine!" he shouted

back from the balcony.

"She needs a psychiatrist, she's demented like her family, she was dragged up from filth, the lazy scrounging bastard!" He was just ranting, on and on.

Those poor people must have thought he was drunk and they went back to their room. But he wasn't drunk, he was just *him*, the bullying, controlling, selfish, uncaring person I had married.

In the morning, I went to see how Alice was. She had wet the bed, poor thing, which was no surprise. He had caused this, and I never told him because it would be something else he'd blame me for. How I wanted him to know that, apart from what he was doing to me, he was harming his children, too. And that is unforgivable.

David was quiet and withdrawn that day, and Alice was upset and humiliated. I reassured her that only I knew what had happened, but it didn't make her feel any better. As for me, I was racking my brain to find a way to get us out of this mess. So much harm was being done, and I only had myself to blame.

My credit card had been damaged in a faulty checkout machine just before we left for the holiday and I hadn't had time to get a replacement, so I had no means of paying for anything. I thought about calling someone at home to ask them to pay for flights for me and the children to get us back to the UK, but that would cost hundreds and I had no way of repaying anyone that kind of money. I checked the safe in our room where John had put all the cash he'd brought for us to use for holiday expenses: it wasn't in there and I knew he had been one step ahead of me again.

Something else was wrong. I was feeling like I couldn't breathe properly. Not the mild asthma I suffered from now and again, this was different. I thought I felt a lump in my airways. I tried not to panic, but suddenly the thought of me dying and having to leave the children with that monster who was their father, made me take action. I woke John and told him I was having a problem. He laughed in my face, of course.

"I know where the doctors are," he said condescendingly, "You admit right now that you have mental health problems and I'll take you. God knows, you really need help, woman."

We all trundled down to the surgery and John came in to the consulting room with me. I explained that I did have mild asthma and perhaps needed a nebuliser, but the doctor examined me and said it wasn't that at all.

"You are experiencing anxiety and stress, my dear, and probably panic attacks as well," he told me, and John couldn't wait to chip in, expressing his agreement with the diagnosis. So, now he had heard it from an expert, and, in his eyes, I was a certified nutcase because I was suffering with mental health problems. The irony of it didn't pass me by. This was just what he had wanted and he was *never* going to let it drop. I had fallen right into his plan to make *me* out to be the mad one in this relationship. Now he had proper evidence.

The doctor prescribed Valium for me to take for the duration of the holiday, and told me to see my own GP back at home. I took the medication and slept a lot. The children were concerned about me but I just needed to get us all through these two weeks. Every time I woke up, I could hear John ranting on and on, to nobody in particular. He was completely deranged and I found it very frightening.

We carried on going down for meals separately, with John at his own table, chuntering away to himself about what a mad wife he had and what a mad, filthy family he'd married into. I could see the looks on other people's faces and I just hoped they didn't realise he was anything to do with us. His behaviour remained the same throughout the entire holiday.

I didn't call Michael back about the twins, but left it until I was back home. I promised myself that was the last time I'd go away with John.

I swore to myself that this was definitely the end of the marriage. We had endured hell at his hands, in one of the most fabulous places you could wish to be in, but we weren't even allowed to enjoy that.

Enough was enough.

…………………

Intense anger and frustration at this latest twist of fate consumed me. How had John managed to come out of it scot-free, while I was diagnosed and put on medication, making it look like I was the one with mental health problems?

For pity's sake, it wasn't me who needed treatment – *he* was the one with the twisted mind.

As soon as we were back home, I contacted the police, and court orders were issued against John to keep him away from the house, away from me and the children. I was desperate for us to feel safe.

Then John did what he did best. He manipulated the situation with his lies and deceit, his apologies and declarations of change and better things ahead, his promises for a wonderful future. And all of this intertwined with the most subtle underlying messages of how dreadful my life would be without him.

I dropped the case and we carried on, but I never lost the feeling of being trapped.

Chapter 23: Worst Nightmare

When little Alice was nine years old, something happened that put even the worst of what had gone before into perspective.

I'd noticed she had a spot on her face that had been there for some time and she kept picking at it, so I'd been buying medicated plasters and headbands to try to heal it and to get her to stop touching it. The more she'd been picking, the more angry it appeared.

One evening, Alice didn't eat much dinner and said she felt ill. I checked her temperature and was shocked at how high it was, and she was starting to look quite out of sorts. After a dose of medicine to bring the temperature down, I got her settled in the spare room with me, and I stayed with her all night.

The morning arrived to find a very poorly little girl, so I put her and David in the car and drove straight to our GP surgery. John had gone off to work early, as usual, so he didn't know anything was wrong. The doctor took one look at Alice and called for an ambulance – that's when I felt really scared. And, once again, I was alone to deal with something really serious.

My little girl lay in the big hospital bed, her sweet face swollen like a balloon, and all you could see were the tubes and suspended plastic bags of antibiotics and various drips, the monitoring machines with their neat rows of lights blinking and that mind-numbing beep, beep, beep. Nurses were scurrying here and there, taking her pulse and temperature, checking her heartbeat, making notes and then scurrying away again. I felt useless.

I was praying, asking God to help my little girl, telling Him how sorry I was for allowing things to get this bad, begging for forgiveness and for the life of my child.

The doctor came in and took hold of my arm, turning me away from the bed. He looked me straight in the eyes and told me the news.

"Alice has a condition called cellulitis. At the moment, it's only affecting her face and we are doing everything we can to treat it."

"So... how serious is it?"

"Well, in the most severe cases, the patient could develop meningitis or septicaemia, but we are confident that we have the condition under control now, so please do try to stay positive."

I had to ring my friend Lisa to ask if she could possibly pick David up and take him to school for me. She didn't hesitate to help out.

Alice's condition had developed so quickly from that single spot, it was terrifying. She was very poorly and lay there, unconscious for most of the time, while I sat beside her bed, unable to do anything for her. I tried ringing John a few times but he didn't want to know, and all I got from him was a curt "She'll be fine".

He had some big business deal going on, so he was too tied up with that to come and see his little girl.

Alice's condition deteriorated even further and the doctor increased her antibiotics to the strongest a child could be given. Her veins kept collapsing and in the end she had fluids going in through her little feet. I was consumed with worry and fear.

In the whole two weeks that our daughter lay critically ill in hospital, her father visited twice, for a very short time on both occasions, and I stayed there for the entire time, only leaving her bedside to take a quick shower or to grab a bite from the café, when either a nurse or another child's parent would kindly sit with her for me.

John's absence didn't go unnoticed. Some of the staff and other parents made little comments, because they could see how I was struggling on my own with the constant worry and lack of sleep. I must have looked dreadful, but everyone was so kind.

"It's not fair that your husband can't support you – you look worn out, you poor thing." And so on.

Of course, they were right. But my priority was Alice and no parent ever felt as grateful as I did when the doctor told me she was out of danger and was actually recovering.

When we were back home, John showed no

interest in Alice's after-care and – of course – never asked if I was OK, if there was anything he could do to help... he just carried on as if nothing had happened. He didn't even bother to look at the giant Get Well card that had arrived from Alice's school pals.

Nothing ever touched him emotionally, not even almost losing his little girl.

Chapter 24: Two Funerals and a Wedding

My dear, sweet Grandma was becoming an old lady. I'd never confided in her about my domestic situation, but she was no fool. She would have known that I wasn't happy with John and I'm certain it would have caused her much sadness.

Considering that my mum, her daughter, had died at the age of forty-two, it was amazing how Gran survived for as long as she did. I was always grateful to have her in my life well into my adult years, and the children loved her very much.

Sadly, when she was ninety-five years old, she passed away and I was, once again, faced with my husband's hatred of my family. He couldn't even manage to control his feelings when someone died, he just had to have a go. It was all about him, always, even when I was preparing for the funeral.

"Seeing that fucking family of yours tomorrow! All

the fucking losers and scumbags will be there, all mean bastards together! Not a decent one among them!"

And, as always, money was brought into it. "I bet you don't get a single penny from your grandmother's death – they never do anything properly, giving it all away to some nursing home instead of you. None of you were brought up properly!" His rage was all-consuming.

With that outburst, he came across the kitchen to where I was standing at the sink unit, and gripped my arms tightly, pressing his fingers into my flesh, then he kicked me on the shin for good measure. I turned towards him to twist out of his grip, but he just laughed and spat in my face.

"That should keep you away from those lot! You're not going tomorrow, and that's that!"

I was sobbing by now, partly with the pain and partly at my feeling of impotence, my inability to fight him. "I love my Gran and she looked after me when my mum died... how can you say that? I'm going, and the children are coming with me."

His seething anger was boiling over, about to explode, and he launched himself at me with all of his weight, pinning me against the worktop. I tried to get him off but he wouldn't budge. He was on my back, weighing me down so I couldn't move, and, no matter how I shouted at him to get off, he just kept lurching forward, pinning me down even more.

David must have heard the commotion and he came into the kitchen. He grabbed hold of John's arms, wrestling his dad off me until I was free. The poor boy was so used to this and he always came to my defence, whereas Alice would run upstairs at the first sign of violence, saying she couldn't do anything.

"You decided to stay with him, Mum. This is what you've chosen to live like, how you choose to be treated." She was right. This was down to me, no-one else.

I did go to the funeral. Grandma had lived a good life for all of those years and that was something to be celebrated. It was also a chance for me to meet up with family again. It was a happy event.

Nobody asked where John was. They just knew he would never be at any family celebrations or events, whether it was a birth, a death, a marriage or anything else. He simply didn't care and he hated every single member of my family. That's a lot of hate.

He despised them for reasons that didn't really exist. He always tried to run them down, make out they were poor, uneducated, a waste of space. And yet, every single relative of mine owned his or her own home, most had been educated at university, and all had successful careers. He was deluded, and I found it bizarre that he was so *obsessed* with them. It was strange.

The funeral was a wonderful send-off for a wonderful lady, and David and Alice enjoyed meeting up with their cousins over a lovely meal at a country hotel.

"How come Dad gets it so wrong about your family?" David asked me.

"I don't think we'll ever know the answer to that," I replied.

…………………

It was springtime, the season of new beginnings and new hopes. An invitation arrived in the post, for Leo's wedding.

It was to be a vintage style event, with a barn dance and a barbecue after the ceremony. But, for me, this little piece of card could only mean trouble.

Over the weeks leading up to the happy day, all I heard was "Fucking mean bastards! Won't even pay for a proper wedding reception! Cunts, the lot of them! My kids aren't mixing with those people! Your dad's an imbecile, a cross-breed!" and so on, without let-up.

This tirade went on for weeks, and any joy I'd felt for my half-brother and his bride-to-be was ground down to the point where I thought maybe it would be best for me not to go to the wedding.

John's behaviour followed the usual pattern of plant-pot hurling across the driveway, and various things being thrown at walls inside the house.

The evening before the big day, the phone rang. It was my aunt, checking to make sure everything was OK for the next day. John exploded and slammed the phone down on her. She rang back, so then he smashed the phone against the wall.

"We don't need that filth in this house! And you can forget going to that cunt's wedding!"

With that, he kicked me hard in my thigh. I

screamed out in pain. David and Alice came running downstairs to see John punching me in the chest and arms. It was agony, and I suddenly thought, *Is this it? Am I going to die just because I want to go to a family wedding?*

When he realised the children were witnessing his violence against me, John shouted, " Look at your mother! She just attacked me and I've had to protect myself! She's gone mad – she needs help, a psychiatrist. Don't go with your mad mother to this wedding!"

The door slammed and he'd left – gone to the pub, no doubt. The children helped me up and into the lounge and I sat there, crying and feeling hopeless and helpless. But I was more determined than ever now to be there for Leo's special day.

We did make it to the wedding, me and the children. I was badly bruised and popping painkillers, but at least I was there. I felt uncomfortable because I was dressed strangely for a wedding, with a big pashmina wrapped around me, covering the bruises on my arms and chest, and my tights were thick and dense black to hide the marks on my legs. Dancing was very difficult and painful, but I made an effort, because I knew what John would have wanted – me injured and unable to join in with the others. I wouldn't give him the satisfaction.

And where was my husband while I fought to feel like celebrating? He'd taken his mother out for dinner.

....

Over time, I had managed to rebuild my relationship with Dad and Shirley, especially once my nephews had moved out of their home and gone back to live with their parents, so there was much more free time and less to do. We would meet up, always in town, and we never once mentioned John. There was no point.

Happily, Dad was retired now and the two of them were busy making plans to see the world after being so tied up looking after the children for years. It was lovely to see them looking forward to their adventures and being able to enjoy their time together. They had already been to the States and were now talking about Australia, New Zealand, the Caribbean... it all sounded fabulous.

Dad was fit and healthy, and he'd recently been to his GP for a full check-up so he knew his blood pressure and cholesterol were as they should be. Volunteering with the local Scout group and playing some indoor sports with friends of his were keeping him in trim. All in all, it pleased me to see him looking forward to a happy and healthy retirement.

Something else he'd started doing was tracing our family tree, both on his side and on Mum's, and he'd managed to go back hundreds of years. Whenever we'd meet, he'd bring along the latest information so we could chat through whatever interesting finds he'd unearthed. It was very exciting, and made for great conversation over coffee and cake. I was so happy – and relieved – that I really had my dad back again.

We all laughed to see the evidence that, on Mum's

side, we'd been related somehow to the royal family – many moons ago and only very distantly, mind you, but what a conversation for future dinner parties!

One summer's day, we were sitting outside the coffee shop enjoying our chat and Dad produced my rather late birthday gift that he'd kept forgetting to bring with him, and no way would he or Shirley ever post anything to me at the house. He'd been so distracted by the successful family tree hunting, he never thought about it. We joked that it was his age and his memory must be slipping.

The gift was a book that I'd wanted for ages and he'd remembered I'd mentioned it, bless him. Once I'd unwrapped it and thanked them both, Dad took out a pen and wrote in the front:

To my Darling Paula,

Happy Birthday

Love from Dad & Shirley XX

The next day, he was dead.

It was eight o'clock in the morning and I was helping David get his kit ready for school. Alice was away on a school trip for the week. John was, as usual, still in bed. The phone rang.

It was Michael, my brother. His voice almost screamed down the line at me, "Dad's dead!"

"No! He can't be... I was with him and Shirley

yesterday... they're both fine... it's a mistake..."

"No! It's true! Here..." There was a crackling noise then a stranger's voice spoke to me, calmly and quietly.

"Paula, my name is Richard – I'm a paramedic. I'm afraid what your brother said is true. Your father passed away a few minutes ago, and we believe it was a massive heart attack but we'll know more later."

I heard myself scream, an awful sound from right down, deep inside me. I rebelled as loud as I could at the bloody injustice of it. How could this be? My dad was the kindest, most gentle soul on earth and he didn't deserve to die like this, too soon, too sudden. It couldn't be true.

I said I'd be with them as quickly as I could. David ran upstairs to tell his dad the awful news.

I knew better than to expect sympathy from John – or anything, really. This was the day when I became an orphan, when I no longer had parents. I had lost them both, much too soon.

John suddenly came rushing down the stairs, like a child on Christmas morning. He was punching the air in his unhinged excitement, and he was shouting – not in anger like normal, but with absolute glee.

"Woo-hoo! He's dead! The cunt's gone and died! Best news I've heard in ages!"

I wasn't in any mood to respond and, anyway, what would be the point? He was heartless. His children had just lost their dear grandfather and he was celebrating. Despicable.

No matter what the circumstances in or around the

family, my whole life with John was a battle, with him constantly attacking – whether that was verbally, physically, mentally or emotionally – and me trying to defend myself. He saw me as a target, something to be subjected to his unreasonable and relentless behaviour. Trying to fight against such an adversary, especially when I was emotionally drained by personal loss, grief... just stripped away every scrap of my humanity.

I told David he could come with me to Dad's house or he could go to school, whichever he preferred. His class were having a Fun Day, which, although seemingly inappropriate, might help him. The poor boy was in shock but he said he'd go to school and come home early. As long as I didn't have to leave him with his uncaring father, I didn't mind what he did.

Shock is a strange thing. I was doing everything on auto-pilot, without really experiencing the actions. I know I shouldn't have driven, and if I'd had a husband with a scrap of human decency, I wouldn't have had to, but I got in the car and somehow arrived at Dad's house, feeling very shaky.

Seeing a police car outside, the reality of what had happened hit me like walking into a door. Apparently, when there is a sudden death, the police are called out as a matter of procedure.

We sat in the lounge in total silence, all crying and in disbelief. We were surrounded by Dad's things: his chair, his pullover draped across the arm, his books, and there was the beautiful picnic set his work colleagues had presented him with on his retirement, for him and Shirley to use on the happy days out they were planning.

Eventually, I asked Shirley what had happened and she said Dad had got out of bed, come downstairs to make some tea, and just fell down, and that was it. Just like that. She had called a neighbour who they were friendly with, and he had tried CPR until the ambulance arrived, but it was no good. Dad was gone.

Shirley had lost her husband and her retirement partner, I'd lost my beloved Dad, and my children had lost their dear grandfather. And my husband was delighted.

Wearing my dark glasses so she wouldn't see I'd been crying, I went to collect Alice from the coach station later, and waited to hear all her news of the week away before I told her, once we were back at the house. She was devastated, and we cried together.

That evening, John went down to the village pub – to celebrate.

The post-mortem showed that Dad had, in fact, died from a massive heart attack, just like Mum had.

Now, they were together again, and I had lost them both.

We buried Dad beside his parents, dressed in his favourite smart suit, just like he would have wanted.

David and Alice asked John to come to the funeral, and he did. But he muttered under his breath through the whole service, and he only spoke once, to my aunt, to tell her he wanted us all dead.

That evening, he went to Dad's newly dug grave,

stepped on to the mound of soil and jumped up and down on the fresh, damp earth. When he returned home, he proudly showed us the mud on his shoes.

Then he laughed, right in our faces.

Chapter 25: Taking Stock

"Keep breathing," I'd tell myself, "something has got to give."

I knew, without any shadow of doubt, that I was married to a man who was severely mentally unstable. He was unpredictable, his mood could change in an instant from extremely positive and seemingly happy, to dark and violent, more often than not with absolutely no provocation.

This was the biggest part of my dilemma. If you are in a relationship with a well adjusted partner, and you come to a point where you both accept that things aren't working, then, OK, it's never easy, but at least you can sort things in a sane and sensible manner.

My position was that I was trapped, and every time I tried to do anything to free myself and the children from this dreadful life, it backfired on me.

I lived in constant fear and dread, walking on eggshells in case I accidentally annoyed John. Knowing he could flip at any second for no reason caused me endless stress, always having to be alert for the next attack, the next abuse.

I had moved myself into the big spare room and put a lock on the door. Alice had a lock on her bedroom door as well. What a terrible statement.

What I couldn't understand was, why did John appear to want to keep me there? Wouldn't it be easier for him just to let me go? Surely he couldn't be happy with this awful existence? Was it a part of his personality disorder that he needed someone to control, to manipulate, someone to feed his evil need to harm and destroy? Why didn't he want to make a clean break and find someone he could be happy with? How could anyone want to carry on like this?

I was going to say, *how could anyone in their right mind want to carry on like this?* But there it is, the explanation.

And that's exactly how it was. John wouldn't even discuss our failed marriage, our domestic madness – he ignored all of it and just went about his business as if nothing was wrong.

I did try to get away, of course I did. I tried the legal route, more than once, and the police were involved, bringing charges against him for the attacks on me, and I was repeatedly granted a Non-Molestation order and an Occupation order by the court.

But, each time I tried, John would manage to wriggle his way out of everything and get off scot-free.

Firstly, he had his 'pet' solicitor, who I'm convinced was afraid of John for some reason, and who was certainly being paid very well to get him out of every situation.

The letters I would receive from this chap always took the same tack: he would accuse *me* of everything John had been guilty of. According to him, I had behaved like a mad woman and attacked John for absolutely no reason, using extreme violence so that he had had no option but to defend himself, and that would explain the bruises I had shown to the police. And so on.

These letters were also quite threatening. Menacing, to be honest. On one occasion, when I had taken the children to get away from John's latest explosion of violence, this solicitor warned me not to take the children "from the family home" again.

Completely separate from this 'legal protection' John appeared to have orchestrated for himself, there were his own on-going threats. When I had returned to the house after one such episode, he told me that, if I ever tried anything like that again, he would kill my family and that I would meet with 'an unfortunate accident'.

And so, charges were dropped and then John carried on as if nothing had ever happened.

I know, to most normal people, that seems ridiculous, something you'd see in a film or read in a novel. But, when you are the person whose life is being controlled by a violent partner who seems to recognise no boundaries at all, and who appears hell-bent on inflicting as much suffering and misery on you as he or she can, you realise that these are not just words of fiction.

I knew by now that John was capable of almost anything, and I would often question the possibility that he might actually kill me one day. It does happen.

Facts. According to the Office of National Statistics, in the year to March 2017, 1.2 million women in England and Wales experienced domestic abuse, and seven women were *killed every month* by their partner or ex-partner.

To add to my already overwhelming fear, as I secretly researched mental health, personality disorders, domestic violence and so on, I came across a terrifying piece of information. The most common method of killing a partner or spouse was recorded as stabbing with a knife. It hit me like a brick that most of John's outbursts took place in the kitchen.

Even worse for me was to read that the second most common method was quoted as 'kicking or hitting'.

More than once, during one of John's attacks, when I was trying to shield myself from the punches and kicks, I believed that, if he didn't stop soon, I would be dead.

Another controlling aspect was that John had gradually manipulated our affairs so that I ended up with no money of my own. From owning my own home and car, and earning a salary, I was now technically penniless.

I would daydream about getting hold of some real cash, even though there was no way that could happen, and taking the children abroad, away from him and this life. Somewhere he couldn't get to us.

But something so drastic would have caused all sorts of havoc. The children's education would be disrupted and that would possibly have a negative effect on their progress, we would have to break all contact with my family and friends, we would have to change our names, live among strangers... the prospect was too daunting, especially for someone who was already very worn down.

It was just a daydream, an escape for a few moments amid the turmoil and chaos.

In short, I had no choice but to stay until I could either find or engineer some way to get out for once and for all time. I needed to be sure that the children and I would be free from John and his threats, his control, and that we wouldn't be left with nothing. For myself, that didn't really matter – but the children deserved better.

I feared that David would copy his father's behaviours and bad habits, but as he grew I could see that he was more like me, showing a gentle, caring nature. He had seen a lot of what John was capable of doing, and he would sometimes speak his mind, telling his dad that he shouldn't be violent and aggressive, but John would make light of every criticism of his treatment of me, saying, "Oh, that's just your mad mother!" Always belittling me, never accepting that anything he was doing was wrong.

Alice really did begin to show that she was

struggling, becoming very withdrawn at times. I would take her into town for a change of scenery, and to get her away from where life was constantly thrown into chaos, and we'd shop for new clothes, have lunch – just ordinary things, my attempt at grabbing a bit of normality, thinly disguised as a girlie day out. We both needed the respite, however brief.

We were wandering around one of the big stores when Alice suddenly stopped dead and began gasping, taking gulps of air and saying she wanted to get outside. The colour drained from her little face and by now I was really concerned. Luckily, the car was parked close by and I drove straight to the hospital, where they rushed her into the children's emergency unit.

Lots of tests were carried out, and all I could do was watch and wait. Being a trained nurse, I knew what they were checking for, and it scared the hell out of me. After what seemed ages, I was advised that Alice was fit and healthy, but had suffered a rather severe panic attack. The doctor asked me if I had any idea what could have brought it on. Of course I knew, but I couldn't tell. He told me I needed to keep a check on her emotional health.

Feeling even more guilty and full of self-loathing, I had to tell John what had happened, although I don't know why I bothered because he just laughed the whole incident away, telling Alice, "It's your mother who should have been in hospital – she's the damaged one!" He really didn't care about anyone or anything – even his little children.

I hated him, even more than I hated myself.

My nights were regularly interrupted by bad dreams, almost every night, possibly partly a side-effect of the anti-anxiety medication I was taking. One dream was that we had a dog, a small, friendly chap with a thick white coat. The children were happy in this dream and spent a lot of time playing with their pet, almost carefree. John wasn't part of this particular dream.

Waking the next morning, I recalled the whole dream vividly, and was suddenly consumed with determination to find a dog for us to adopt. Taking David and Alice with me, I drove to our nearest RSPCA centre, only to discover we were there before they opened, so we waited by the car.

As we stood there, a car pulled up near us. The man driving had a little boy with him, and a tiny white dog, a very young Westie pup. The man told us they were going to leave the dog at the centre because he couldn't look after it any longer, due to his marriage breaking up – it was a really sad tale. He seemed genuine, and rather lost and forlorn.

The little boy was crying, heartbroken at the thought of having to say goodbye to his puppy, but his dad was adamant about it. They simply couldn't afford to keep any pets right now. The whole thing was terribly sad. I bent down and picked the little dog up, and a warm tongue licked my face, making me laugh.

Alice squealed with delight as our new pal gave me a thorough wash, and the little boy looked up at me. "You will look after him, won't you?"

Then he reached into the car and brought out a small dog bed and a carrier bag. "Here's his bed and his toys, and his name's Alfie."

We all promised we would take great care of Alfie and assured the unhappy child that his pet would have a nice new home and that he would definitely be loved. I took twenty pounds out of my purse and handed it to the boy, who wiped his tear-stained face and smiled at me, with a very polite "Thank you".

Alfie was taken to the vet the next day and had a thorough check-up, including flea treatment for his infestation. That made me realise how that poor man must have been struggling to look after the pup and deal with the break-up with his wife, as well as having a small child to care for. My heart went out to the little boy, watching his mummy leave and then having to let his special furry friend go. How unfair it all was.

Alfie brought something into our home that was truly wonderful. Much-needed love. Naturally, John wasn't happy about the addition to the family, but he chose to ignore the little bundle of cuteness and never once bothered with him.

I couldn't believe that I had actually done this, but it felt really good! And some time later, I took in a Jack Russell, a little girl called Rosie. In the meantime, all I could do was try to keep the peace, not do anything to wind John up, hold my tongue when I really wanted to scream in his face, and keep the children as safe as I could.

It was the most difficult challenge of my life.

Chapter 26: Revelations

The situation was untenable, so uncomfortable and stressful, I did start to drink more and – surprise, surprise – I found I was putting on weight. I realised I was also comfort eating, but by now I was too far down to try to do anything about it. If it helped me get through this, then so be it.

Of course, that just gave John another reason to mock me constantly. So now, not only was I thick, useless, a religious nutter, and badly brought up, as well as completely mad, I was also a big fat pig! Although I knew I was heavier, I reached ten and a half stone at the most, and that's fine for my height.

John carried on, going out in the evenings and at weekends when he wasn't working. If I ever asked him where he'd been, I'd get the same retort, which he would spit at me as he pushed past and elbowed me out of the way. "Nothing to do with you."

I began to wonder if he was actually seeing another woman. And, if that was the case, why didn't he just tell me we were finished? Why would he want to keep me there if he really was starting to build a new life for himself? He was certainly behaving like a man having an affair, but surely the John I knew would be flaunting that in my face?

It was all so confusing, but I did at least begin to get the feeling that things would have to change soon.

David told me something that took this line of thought a little further. He'd got into his dad's car and opened the glove compartment. Inside was a packet of condoms. Of course, John told him they weren't his, and that they belonged to his friend who'd had a lift in the car recently.

The trouble with this was that it wouldn't surprise me to find out John had purposely planted them there so that David would see them and it would get back to me. But why would he do that? To make me jealous? Maybe he wasn't seeing someone, maybe he was hoping I'd be so unhappy to think he'd found someone else, I'd declare my undying love for him and pop back to the marital bed.

I gave up trying to work out what his motives were – it was way too complicated and I'm pretty certain it would have driven me as mad as he was if I carried on!

John would frequently taunt me when he was going out, reminding me how successful he was, how wealthy, how slim and attractive to women. "I can easily find someone much better than you! Someone gorgeous and skinny!" To be honest, I wished he would.

He started going on holidays on his own. Those times became something to look forward to, to be enjoyed and relished. It was just me and the children, peace and quiet, lovely chats and laughter – yes, laughter would once again fill the spaces of our house. And we would do exactly what we wanted to do, without fear of criticism, or worse.

Of course, he'd eventually return and then I'd hear all about the fabulous women he'd met, how they were wealthy and successful – just like him! And, naturally, they were all perfectly beautiful with amazing figures.

I honestly never knew if he was being truthful or not. In fact, part of me wished he *would* meet someone, then surely he'd want to sort out this sham of a marriage and get on with his new life.

As much as I played my role of housekeeper and mother, cooking nice meals and never complaining or criticising, every now and then John's dark side would leap into the limelight and there would be another violent attack. I tried really hard to defend myself but he overpowered me every time.

When there wasn't physical abuse, I'd be on the receiving end of his verbal attacks, but by now I could cope with those, and his words, after so many repetitions, started to lose their meaning to me. It was just noise.

I kept believing – assuming – that, to the outside world, we appeared as a normal, well adjusted and happy little family. How naïve I was.

I was walking the dog one morning when I

bumped into our neighbour, Marion, and we stopped to chat. As I was telling her that Alice's school exams were coming up soon, she reached up her hand and lifted my sunglasses. I had a nasty black eye from the latest confrontation.

"Please don't even try to defend John to me." Her voice was full of sympathy, understanding, and it shocked me. "There aren't many people around here with a good word to say about him."

I was speechless. I'd always imagined him down the village pub, chatting and laughing with all the locals, being everyone's pal and a real ladies' man. And now I'm hearing that nobody likes him.

It was one of those 'shall I laugh or cry?' moments, but the combination of Marion's sympathy and the sudden realisation of John's lack of popularity seemed to open a floodgate. I could barely speak because I was crying so much.

Marion took me into her house and made tea. I calmed down a bit and we chatted over several cups. The relief of being able to speak openly and honestly to another human being, instead of always having to keep up the pretence, was incredibly uplifting and comforting. I could feel the pent-up fear and stress, and all of those other screwed-up emotions, fall away. It was like seeing daylight after a long time in the dark.

John always told me that no-one would ever believe me if I was stupid enough to talk about how things really were behind our closed doors. And yet, here I was, sitting with this lovely lady, learning that

John was *not* the publicly adored hero he would have me believe. What a turn-up for the books, as they say!

The part of this that was really funny was that he had caused this to happen, by giving me a black eye. He normally hit me on the arms, legs and body, where I could easily cover up any bruising and suffer in silence. But just lately he seemed to be losing control even more than before and he'd just lash out, hitting me in the face.

More fool him. Although the eye hurt and I was ashamed to be John's punch-bag, what came from this was making me see things in a very different light.

Chapter 27: A Rock and a Hard Place

All of this 'keeping my head down' and playing the dutiful wife in order to keep the peace – or what little peace we could manage – meant that I still had to go along with those 'family plans' of John's that I really wanted to avoid. Like holidays.

It was one thing having John kicking off in our own home, but having to try to deal with him in hotels and restaurants, surrounded by total strangers, was something else altogether.

A decision was made to sell the boat that was lying more or less unused on the east coast. Alice and David were disappointed, but they perked up when John announced that we were to have a family break in the Lake District. They both loved climbing with their dad, and it meant that I could grab some precious 'me time' while they were off exploring. There was no way I wanted to be halfway up a mountain with John, no thanks.

Although a pretty dismal failure as a husband, John

had never shown any inclination to hurt the children, so it didn't cause me any worry in that respect to leave them with him. I was totally aware that his on-going abhorrent behaviour was not something they should have had to witness, but I did believe that, without me there, he wouldn't need to switch to 'nasty John' – and I knew beyond doubt that the children needed to have a relationship with their father.

The journey was always a bad experience. David would want to be the navigator and so would sit in the front passenger seat, leaving me to sit in the back with Alice. John would shout and swear for the entire distance between home and our destination, telling the children what a 'low-life' their mother was. It sounds ridiculous now, but that's exactly how it was.

I'm sure David and Alice learned somehow to switch off from it, or filter some of it out, and once Alice fell asleep without realising she'd left her mobile switched on *and still connected to the friend she'd been chatting with*. We later found out that the poor girl had heard John's ranting for a couple of hours! She was horrified.

John would often pull up on the hard shoulder, get out of the car and have a pee, just standing there in full view of everyone going past. Drivers would sound their horns at him and shake their fists in his direction, but he couldn't care less. "Wankers!" he'd shout back at them. A law unto himself.

One of my personal favourite places in the Lake District has always been Borrowdale. Hardly any signs of civilisation, and those that do exist simply blend in with the fells, the breath-taking views, the rivers and waterfalls. In Grange, a few tiny stone-built cottages with overflowing gardens nestle at the foot of the mighty fells, the sparkling river running gently under a curved stone bridge that leads you to a tiny tea shop offering home-made cakes and local ice cream. Just along the road, the lapping shingle shores of Derwentwater, as the lake opens wider and wider until it reaches the little wooden piers where the Keswick motor launches take smiling tourists all round the lake's edge. Such a magical place.

Fortunately, Borrowdale is one of the best places for rock climbing, so it was equally John's choice for a place to stay. One morning, after a fabulous Northern breakfast, we all put our walking boots and shorts on, popped essentials in our backpacks and set off for a day in Keswick. The sun was shining, it was warm without being too hot, and John appeared to be in a calm mood.

We found a space in the open-air car park close to the market square and I went to get a ticket for the whole day's stay. Suddenly, David started talking about his uncle Leo, my half-brother. I stopped dead in my tracks, my heart now racing.

The children both understood that we *never* spoke about my family in front of their father, and I couldn't for the life of me work out why David was doing this, especially as John had been in such a good mood up to that point. I held my breath and very gingerly placed the parking ticket on the windscreen.

What happened next was terrifying. John launched

at me, grabbed me round the throat with both hands and started squeezing with all of his might. His face was dark red, contorted with sheer rage, and the veins in his forehead were bulging from under the skin.

He kept squeezing, I couldn't breathe and I was choking, trying to cough, trying to push him away but I had no strength... I felt myself losing consciousness as I made my weakened efforts to loosen John's grip. The children were screaming at him to let me go...

I could see people all around the busy car park, staring at us, and I tried to scream for help, but no sound came out. Nobody came near. I was losing all of my senses. "Dad! Stop it!" The children were sobbing now.

Time seemed to stretch somehow as I felt weaker and weaker, losing my connection to reality. Then – I have no idea why – John released his hold on me and I slumped to the ground, gasping and choking, trying desperately to breathe in, to get air into my lungs again. My head was pulsing and my limbs were useless, like a rag doll.

Shock. Disbelief. My husband had just tried to strangle me in a crowded public place in broad daylight, and in front of our children. For absolutely no good reason. I couldn't think straight.

Eventually, with the help of the children, I picked myself up, took my bag from the car and led them into the nearest tea shop, almost falling into a chair by the window. We sat silently, drinking hot chocolate and sharing a big slab of home-made gingerbread.

I saw John walk off towards the fell, and he was still clearly shouting his usual obscenities as he went.

David told me there was an open-top bus that travelled between Keswick and Borrowdale regularly, so we knew we could get back to the guesthouse. We spent some time sitting there, just recovering from what had happened, with me silently thanking God that I was still alive, and after a while we made our way back on the bus.

All of this natural beauty, tranquillity and peace, and yet, what we were living through was nothing but pure evil.

Chapter 28: The Fallout

So many times, I'd imagined how it would be, in that new future, our new existence after John had gone and we would be free to live our lives.

There would be calm, order and tranquillity – it would be wonderful. We would talk together, about anything and everything, and we'd laugh, probably at nothing very much. And, best of all, we'd have peace of mind without the fear, the worry, without that constant, unrelenting, nerve-jangling dread that the devil himself is about to grab you and drag you down to his hell.

But the reality of those first few days after John's arrest on Alice's birthday was very different. The atmosphere in the house was highly charged, and all three of us were in a state of being overwhelmed by our emotions. It was a distressing time.

My priority, above and beyond everything else, was my children. David and Alice. Not only had my daughter's coming-of-age celebration been totally destroyed, but now she was facing her A-Level exams and I had no idea how she would get through. The violent scene with her father had left her deep in shock and devastated.

That first morning, I went out to walk the dogs on the park, and a lady was strolling there with her two little dogs. We got chatting and she struck me as having a warm and kindly nature. Maybe because I was in shock, I'm not sure, but I heard myself telling her what had happened. She was my first opportunity to let it all out, God help her, but she listened patiently until I eventually stopped talking.

"You really must have a word with Alice's school. I'm a head teacher myself and I know they'll be able to help. They have properly qualified people who can support her through this by providing some professional support. Believe me, please contact them straight away."

It made sense, and I wondered why I hadn't thought of that. I spoke to the deputy head as soon as I could get an appointment. When I explained, among everything else, that Alice had kept her personal suffering inside and hadn't even confided in her closest friends, there was concern that she might suddenly 'blow', a bit like a pressure cooker, now that the situation had changed. That would not be good for her.

It felt safe to be discussing these things with people who obviously cared, and who had the professional knowledge to actually help. They recommended a psychiatrist who also offered counselling for young adults. The following day, Alice and I were sitting in this lady's consulting room.

Thank heaven for that woman on the park!

We sat there, side by side, and everything came spilling out. The years of abuse – mental, physical and emotional; our nightmares and flashbacks to some of the more extreme incidents; and we both wept uncontrollably.

The psychiatrist explained about PTSD – Post Traumatic Stress Disorder – emphasising that the condition wasn't reserved for soldiers coming out of dreadful war situations after witnessing atrocities that no human should ever see. "You are both experiencing PTSD as a result of the years of violence and abuse," she told us, and I was suddenly engulfed in a sense of guilt, so extreme I started to cough in order to stop myself choking.

I had allowed this to happen. Only me, there was no-one else to blame. How had I let it go on for so long? Why didn't I see it was destroying us? God, I felt so bad.

It was agreed that Alice would be given counselling and support in light of her rapidly approaching exams. She needed absolute peace and a lot of reassurance to help her through this difficult time. Her studies had been badly affected by her father's behaviour – how could she revise, with him constantly shouting and swearing, smashing things and lashing out for no reason? What a bastard he was, to completely ignore the basic needs of his own children. I felt a very real hatred for him.

But, whatever I did or didn't feel for him now, I needed to get a grip. Having been put down and controlled so forcefully for all of that time, I was incredibly weak, an emotional wreck. It took one hell of an effort to summon any strength. Human resilience is an amazing thing, thank heaven.

Chapter 29: Storm Warning

Here we were, at the beginning of our new life, and so far we were having professional counselling, we'd been diagnosed as suffering from PTSD [Post Traumatic Stress Disorder], and I was consumed with guilt. And ahead of us was the prospect of legal proceedings against John, combined with what threatened to be a bitterly contentious divorce.

The village didn't take long to start buzzing with the gossip. I say 'gossip' but it was all true. Everyone knew we had separated and John had moved out into his flashy new place, and people were asking questions. What had happened? Was I alright? Were the children safe? I was at least comforted in the knowledge that no-one knew about the police involvement or the GBH charge, and I really didn't want that getting out. We had to live in this village and it wouldn't be fair to the children to be labelled as being brought up in a dysfunctional and violent home. Even if it were true.

Having said that, I could very happily have

scrambled up on to the roof and screamed it all out loud. I didn't, of course, I just left it for the courts to deal with everything properly, to see that John finally got his just desserts, then we could close the door and move on.

It was reassuring to know that he couldn't come near the house for a full year, thanks to the court order. This twelve months would allow me the time to sort myself out so that I could be there for David and Alice, and to prepare for what was ahead.

David had begun to show just how hard it was all hitting him, now that he knew for certain this was the end of the marriage, the end of our family. He was finding it difficult to see his mother take his father to court, and he hated the idea of us divorcing. He was having frequent nightmares and I was seriously concerned about him.

While his children were suffering from the effects of his ever-worsening control and violence, and struggling to deal with the reality of the situation, John had rented a luxury 'pad' for himself in the newly developed part of the village, and he was carrying on with his own life as if nothing was happening, going out every evening, dressing up in his new designer clothes – and no doubt looking for my replacement. Another vulnerable woman to be his next victim, someone to impress with his successful business and money, and then, once she was hooked, she would be someone to control and abuse. I actually felt sorry for whoever she would be.

In the lead-up to Alice's exams, David and I did what we could to help her study. There was no door slamming, no shouting and swearing, no violent outbursts, and we all commented that we could even hear the birds in the garden as they chirped and whistled – almost as if they appreciated the new atmosphere, too. It was quite strange, but in a good way. The mood in the house took on an aura of respect and calm, with all of us going about our day-to-day activities without holding our breath or looking over our shoulders. It was a revelation, even if it took a bit of getting used to.

I started to lose weight, so my self-esteem slowly began to reappear, which in turn made me feel stronger and more positive, more able to cope and think about things in a more balanced way. I unleashed my housework demons on our home, attacking one room after another, getting rid of things that held bad memories. My personal cleansing ritual.

People commented on how well we were doing – not such a shabby performance for a family suffering from PTSD, anxiety, depression, and goodness knows what else! The sense of relief started tentatively, but it grew and grew, becoming quite exhilarating.

Against all odds, Alice did really well in her exams. It was a wonderful feeling, knowing that John hadn't succeeded in destroying her future. And yet, something was still not right.

Alice had been advised to take a year out before starting university, and she got a job with a holiday company for a few months, which meant living away from home for that time. Although I would have preferred the three of us to be together right now, I did think it was best for her to get away.

Throughout all of the horrors, David had been the strong one, always being there and fighting (literally at times) to keep the family together, regardless of the abuse. Like so many children in abusive family situations, he'd put so much energy into trying to keep things on an even keel and now – well, he must have been mentally and emotionally drained.

Unfortunately, with Alice going away, he felt she'd 'deserted' him and he had no other siblings to turn to. His family, that he'd fought so hard for, was now literally halved, the nest was almost empty and there was the divorce lurking ahead. Somehow, David felt responsible.

Feeling he was losing control, his anxiety level went sky-high, and he began to show symptoms of OCD [Obsessive Compulsive Disorder], when he would fret terribly about doors being locked or appliances switched off. His nightmares continued. It was heartbreaking to see, but he wouldn't even discuss getting some help.

As the summer warmth turned to winter chills, the divorce battle loomed over us like the Grim Reaper and David got badly caught up in it, pushing him even closer to the edge.

Chapter 30: Money Business

The only thing John and I agreed on was that neither of us wanted to get into a divorce battle, but all of our money was tied up in the business and, since I was officially a shareholder and part of the company for over twenty years, this had to be sorted out.

Apparently, there was no cash anywhere else, although, having said that, because John lied so much and had always kept things from me over the years, I honestly couldn't possibly know what the true financial picture was.

John's plan to avoid the huge costly divorce was to attempt to do various 'deals' with me and he was constantly ringing me, offering me yet another scheme, and they were all, according to him, brilliant offers and I'd be a fool to turn them down, etc. Given his track record, how on earth would I have known if anything he was offering was good or bad? This went on for about a year, with him offering one 'deal' after another, each one presumably a better option than its predecessor. He was obviously desperate to get me to agree to something before the courts made their decisions about the financial split.

Friends told me I'd be completely mad to agree to any of this, and they said I should ignore him. But John was nothing if not persistent, and whenever he set out to achieve something, nothing could get in his way. Some of his offers were laughable, like his idea of me living on my own on a boat, moving to a different harbour each month so I could have a different view! I mean, I loved boats, but that was ludicrous. I knew he just wanted me out of the way so he could have 'his' lovely house back and pick up his former lifestyle, but with someone new.

The children and I would have been dead to him.

Then the accountants took over. That's when things were revealed to me that I'd had absolutely no knowledge of, papers I had apparently signed, agreeing to reallocation of funds from one place to another – all things I knew nothing about because of the way John had constantly bullied me into signing documents without allowing me to read them. It was such a shambles.

David was caught in the middle of it all. John made use of that situation, blaming me for everything, telling the poor lad it was my fault we were in this awful mess and that I was refusing to help him resolve everything! He would tell David what a dirty, scrounging piece of filth I was, how thick I was, what a disgrace. Worse than that, he even told our own son that he was going to kill me and my entire family.

He was angry that I wouldn't fall for his schemes and agree to a 'deal'. The legal process moved on, but the divorce couldn't be completed until the money side of things was resolved. It was a most unsettling time for us.

The solicitors were making the most of the situation, and their bills were nothing short of shocking. I'd had to take out a loan to pay my solicitor, on the basis that I'd be able to repay the borrowing once the divorce was finalised. The trouble was, once you've gone so far down this road, you have no option but to carry on, with the bills constantly plopping on the doormat. Now seriously worried about owing such large amounts of money, I would often mentally kick myself as I remembered how financially sorted I'd been when I first met John. I was also beginning to feel depressed.

Eventually, the solicitors decided there should be a court hearing to agree how the money should be split, and a pre-hearing meeting was arranged. This was a couple of days before Christmas.

The sight of my lawyer wheeling in a pile of boxes of case notes made me feel empty and hopeless. Those sad boxes contained my life, my children's lives, the whole of my utterly wretched marriage. There were photos of my many injuries and bruises, dental records, police reports, A & E records... so much misery, all packed up together.

As I walked into the lawyers' office, I saw a

Christmas tree with twinkling coloured lights, and the staff were obviously in festive spirits, laughing and chatting as they prepared for their holiday. But I wasn't feeling festive, I was dreading what I was about to be told – once again, it seemed that my fate was in the hands of others, and this was yet another situation over which I had no control whatsoever.

Shaking and tearful, I listened as they explained what the situation was. I couldn't believe my ears. They were saying that the business would have to be liquidated in order to raise the funds to pay me off in the divorce. *What? How could this be?* No way around it, they said, and the sale of the company would generate a tax liability that would wipe out much of the equity. Including the house.

The house that I'd been led to believe was almost paid off, was actually not even slightly paid for *because John had bullied me into signing a paper ages ago that instructed the transfer of the equity in the house – into the business.*

Merry Christmas.

Chapter 31: Square One Again

Having had it explained to me on so many previous occasions, when John always used the business as the reason why I *should not* take legal action against him, it was well and truly hammered home, and as I sat there, listening to the legal experts telling me the only way the divorce could proceed was by the court enforcing the liquidation of the company, I was stunned, unable to take it in.

My drive home was miserable, the road ahead more blur than tarmac, through the endless tears. My brain wouldn't, couldn't process what I'd been told. I just didn't understand. It was a very successful business, I knew that, and the idea of it having to close down, with the resulting problems for all of us, *just so we could divorce*, was unthinkable.

By this time, even without the actual court case, I'd run up around thirty thousand pounds in solicitors' fees, and the only way I'd ever be able to pay that off would be from the divorce settlement. Was this the ultimate *Catch 22* or what? Without the divorce, there would be no settlement. Without the settlement, I couldn't pay the debt. How could this have happened?

And then it was Christmas Eve. The house suddenly turned very cold and we discovered that the boiler had broken down. It was one of the coldest winters for years. Alice came home and the three of us tried our best to make something of Christmas, but we didn't have the energy and by Boxing Day we were carrying the tree outside, where we planted it in the garden.

My head was reeling with what to do next, and I had a big decision to make – and soon. If I pushed for the divorce, and the business was finished, what then? Or should I stop the court case, cancel the divorce proceedings? But I'd already spent all of that money – money I didn't have. As much as I might hate John for everything he'd put us through, I would be stupid to bite off the hand that fed us all. Surely there was a way around this? Why weren't my lawyers telling me what the answer was? I was having tension headaches from the moment I woke up to the moment, somewhere in the darkly depressing early hours, when, finally exhausted, I closed my eyes.

David made his feelings clear. "If you force the closure of the business, I'll never forgive you!" He and Alice agreed, without doubt, that I should put a stop to all of it and simply remain separated. It seemed that divorcing and working out a financial settlement was impossible.

So, that's exactly what I did. I called the whole

thing off. Even that wasn't easy. The legal team were pressing me to carry on with the case, and it almost had to go that way because of everything being fixed by timescales and deadlines. However, after some nail-biting and breath-holding moments, the decree nisi was revoked and the divorce was cancelled. And, of course, my legal bill was now even higher than before. But I did it for the children: they needed security, a future, a decent life. By God, they deserved that.

As for me, I had a foreboding feeling that I would be tied to John for the rest of my life, one way or another. The worst thing, from my point of view, was that John had got away with everything, that he would have to face no retribution, no justice – he would not have his day of reckoning.

Well, maybe not in this life.

My only consolation was knowing I'd made the right decision, however uncomfortable it might make me. I made my mind up that I would, somehow, find a different way to achieve a more acceptable outcome, but this time without running up a massive debt. There just had to be a better way to do this.

The business settled my legal bills. John and I agreed that I would carry on using the credit card (with the usual controlling terms and conditions, of course), while he would take care of all household bills, and we would carry on with this 'arrangement' until there was a legal financial settlement.

It didn't take long for John to re-start his battle plan, and we seemed to be right back where we started, with him constantly sending text messages and emails, and calling on the phone with the same old abuse. "Get out of my fucking house, you thick peasant! Find your own house and fuck off! The sooner, the better – it's *my* house!"

I didn't retaliate. But I did remind him, quite calmly, that the house was in both our names.

David and I were worn out with it all, and there was never any respite from John's attacks. But there was one thing that had changed, and I wasn't sure whether it was good news – or bad. John had been seeing several women and he didn't seem to worry about people knowing. He told David that a lot of them were too demanding, and he didn't want that level of commitment! He said he wanted to be free, but with a 'token girlfriend'.

As for me, having only just survived the relationship from hell for all of those years, the last thing I wanted to think about was meeting another man. John's actions said a lot about how shallow he was.

Alice's year out was coming to an end, and I felt she was much better now, a lot brighter and more her old self. She was actively making plans for starting university, and had decided she'd like to study Art and European History. Preparations were under way, and we'd go shopping for all the things she'd be needing in her digs, like bedding, crockery and cutlery, and so on. I was so proud of her for overcoming everything to get this far, and I saw it as a momentous achievement.

I drove her up to the university in Nottingham and

we met with some of her new friends. I was happy to share the excitement she was feeling at the prospect of this brave new beginning, a big step forward for her. The flat she was going to be living in was modern, light and airy, in a purpose-built block – and it was in a decent area of the city. Quite a lot of students were moving in, so I knew Alice would easily make friends and not be alone.

We put her things in her room, made up the bed with a pretty duvet set, then went off to the local shops to buy food and supplies. I was truly happy for her.

I thought it best to let her get on with things in her own way while she settled in, so I didn't bother her with too many phone calls, but we kept in touch once a week. I was taking a bit of 'me time' in Stratford-on-Avon a few weeks later when she rang and told me she'd been seeing a psychiatrist and having regular counselling, the whole time she'd been away, because she'd been diagnosed with mental health issues. As she was now over eighteen, no-one had needed to inform me and Alice had asked them not to.

The thought of my little girl suffering on her own in that flat, so far away, filled me with dread, and I was angry that the university hadn't contacted me, or even one of her pals. But she'd told me now, so I drove up to bring her home. We cleared out the flat that had felt so positive last time I was there, and I was devastated to see her clothes and personal things strewn around the floor, with nothing hanging in the wardrobes, nothing folded in the cupboards. The bed was unmade and there were dirty pots in the kitchen – all signs of the depression I now knew she was struggling with.

Although the scene was quite shocking, because I'd believed she was doing OK, it didn't come as a surprise. Now, all three of us were being treated for the after-effects of our life with John, and yet he was behaving as if he was completely unaffected by any of this. What a monster he was.

Alice's counsellor advised her to take a second year out, and she needed little persuasion. She had made a good friend in the first year, a young man named George who had recently come out as gay, and he and Alice had formed a really close friendship. They decided to do some travelling around New Zealand, planning to take casual jobs as they moved around the country. And off they went.

Of course, I missed her dreadfully, but the constant photos they sent showed a happy, smiling girl with her loyal companion who was right by her side, so I knew this was a good thing for her just now. She was on the road to repair and I will always be grateful to George for taking care of my daughter with his warmth and love. His friendship and support played a very big part in Alice's recovery.

For now, I had to set my sights on getting a divorce and a financial settlement, once and for all.

Chapter 32: The Final Resolution

The garden centre was always a place of peace and serenity for me, where I would escape for a while, just to find a little quiet time. I was strolling around, looking at the roses and thinking how it would be nice to have some in our garden, when my mobile rang.

It was John and, as always, he was angry. His voice grated on me down the phone line as I stared at the label on a lovely rose in front of me, named 'Peace'. How ironic.

"Have you fucking decided what date you're moving out of *my house* yet?"

"It's not your house, John, it's in joint names", I told him calmly, and immediately held the phone well away from my ear.

"I'm bloody sick of waiting! You and your shit little life! You need a fucking good kick up the arse! Filthy dirty imbecile! I want to get on with my life!" He was almost screaming at this point.

After everything he'd done, everything he'd got away with – because I'd let him – I was still stunned at his insensitivity and utter selfishness. *His life?* What about *our lives?*

I tried to stay calm. "John, I've decided to stay in the family home because David is too ill to move right now. He needs security, routine and no more stress, certainly not the upheaval of moving home." I repeated the Counsellor's words to him and awaited the next barrage of abuse.

"Well, in that case, you dirty, scrounging bitch, you need to know something – I've met someone amazing!"

My immediate thought was, *who on earth would want this man?* This vile, wicked, selfish, cruel monster who has all but destroyed his own family, and then moved on without a care in the world, to seek out his next victim.

Then I felt a pang of sympathy for this woman, whoever she may be, and I wondered what she was like. Kind? Vulnerable? Maybe with children of her own? God forbid.

He would have won her over with his odd charm, weakened any resolve she might have had, and pursued her with gifts and romantic gestures. I remembered how it had been when I first met him, how hard he tried to win me round, and how I started to believe I'd landed on my feet with him. I wanted to scream at this woman, to tell her to run fast and run far, before it's too late!

I could only imagine the lies he would no doubt be feeding her, about his dreadful marriage to a violent, uncontrollable wife who came from a mad family! He would convince her everything had been my fault, he would tell her she was everything I wasn't – that she was amazing. His voice was still rattling on, but what he said next really stopped me in my tracks.

"I'm giving you permission to go ahead and find yourself someone else – now that I've found someone, it's OK for you to date other people." Gosh, how gracious of him. "By the way, Paula, she's really lovely."

Those last few words shook me badly. How could he say that to me? I hated myself for being affected this way, but anger was surging through me now. He'd called *me* lovely when we first got together, and now *someone else* was lovely. After all he'd done to me and the children, why would anyone want to be lovely to him, when all he deserved was to be punished? I'd let him get away with everything, and for that I was consumed with anger *at myself*.

Now, though, there was something far more important than my mixed-up emotions. Having learned that John had met his 'amazing woman', I knew I needed to get the divorce settled as quickly as possible, because it worried me that he would start moving money around, taking it out of the business, to fudge the true financial situation and protect his own interests. If I knew anything, I knew how capable he was of such trickery.

Getting ready the next morning for my appointment with a new solicitor, I saw the postman coming up the drive. "Morning, Jane!" He was used to handing me official-looking letters by now, but the one on the top seemed to be even more serious than the rest, so I tore it open. In a million years, I could never have guessed what I was about to read.

John was divorcing me!

After all those years of me trying to divorce him, he'd turned the tables on me! This was all the wrong way round, so, so wrong. *He* was making *me* out to be the baddie! Why was there never any justice in this, justice for me and the children? Worse than that was the weight of guilt pressing on me, guilt because I had kept *allowing him to get away with it all*.

I couldn't get my head around it, and felt like the worst person in the world. Even now, after being separated for some time, he was still able to make me suffer.

The solicitor I'd eventually decided to go with was nothing like those barristers who charged the earth but never really got us anywhere; she was kind and seemed to actually understand my situation, instead of just seeing me as another case. Not only that, she was happy to use the preparation work done by the previous legal team, and her aim was to negotiate an amicable divorce with a sensible solution, without courts and high-priced barristers. She also understood my concern that John might start being underhand with the finances, especially now he was playing happy families with his new lady.

I could tell this legal lady was genuinely sympathetic when I poured out the whole sorry saga, and especially when she heard how much I'd spent on trying to get the divorce. But she vowed to help me, and I was confident in her ability and in her understanding of my position.

Her advice was not to bother issuing a counter divorce petition, because that would just run up more expense, causing delays and further problems. "If you truly want to free yourself from this man – and I can see that really is the case – then my advice is to grit your teeth and accept the situation as it stands. The sooner we get on with this, the sooner you can put him, and all that he has done to you, behind you."

That was the most important thing. No matter how wrong it felt, how sad and upset it was making me, I was tired of fighting with the law. So I let it be, and I just had to keep my eye on the goal. It was wrong – John knew that as well as I knew it. Life just isn't fair.

One good thing amid all of the angst was that I'd been attending an excellent group for divorced people, where I met with like-minded men and women, all going through separation and divorce, and all of the accompanying mess involving children, money, property and so on, ad infinitum. I took a lot of comfort from the friendship, support and counselling, for which I was, and always will be, extremely grateful.

Finally, there was a meeting of solicitors and a deal was thrashed out. In the end, it was as simple as that, because all of the groundwork had already been done. I agreed to a consent order that would run over a few years, which allowed the business to carry on trading while paying off the settlement to me.

That was all it took. No court hearings, no barristers with their hefty bills – just common sense. The divorce went through.

Just short of twenty-five years of marriage, gone, ended, finished. But I had my two wonderful children, who had come through the most dreadful childhood years imaginable and now they needed a decent life. I was determined that was what they would have.

On what would have been our twenty-fifth wedding anniversary, at exactly 12 o'clock midday when we had said "I do", I walked into a tattoo parlour and had a small arrow tattooed on my foot, pointing ahead. It is my permanent reminder to keep moving forward, never to look back.

I was free. I could draw a line under everything that had gone before and focus on the future for Alice, David and myself. We all three needed to come to terms with those destructive years, and we needed to heal.

Only time would help us to do that.

Chapter 33: It's All Over Now

It would be easy to imagine, looking in from the outside, that, having finally got the divorce, I would be relieved, free, able to get on with my new life. If only.

For that first year after I received the decree absolute, I was consumed with anger – at so many different aspects of everything that had happened. For a start, I was angry with myself for allowing John to get away with everything he had done to me and our children for all of those years. How could someone treat his own family so dreadfully, with such vile and abusive behaviour, causing injury and trauma, making them constantly nervous and on edge, afraid to speak or move in case they annoyed him – and simply walk away, scot free? How could that happen?

I was angry that justice had not been meted out. The legal experts had done a lot of work, I admit, but they had also charged a lot of money, and at the end of it all, the guilty party didn't have to pay a price for his evil actions.

Far beyond anger was the feeling I experienced

over John divorcing me. That drove me to experience such dreadful frustration, I suffered headaches whenever I allowed myself to think about it, and I would get this awful surge of inner violence through my whole being. I had tried to divorce him so many times, I was the one with all of the grounds for divorce, for pity's sake – physical cruelty, mental cruelty, emotional cruelty, financial misdeeds... it was a long list. And yet, he'd won again and I was made to look like the bad one.

I had saved the business by not pushing for a divorce, and – even more to the point – I'd kept him out of prison! The frustration was indescribable.

As for the new woman in John's life, I had all kinds of feelings towards her, about her taking my place. I'd built up this image of a beautiful, successful, sexy, popular, confident super-model who had stepped into my shoes and who would now be enjoying the spoils of her victory beside the man who would be totally the opposite of the husband I'd lived with. He would be exactly how he was with me in the early days *before he knew I was under his control.*

I imagined the two of them together, laughing and touching, enjoying each other, *being happy*. She would be having the life I should have had, she would get the best of the man who gave me his worst, the man who made my life unbearable.

David eventually met her, and I was – what? relieved? pleased? smug, even? – to learn from him that this 'superwoman' was just a woman. She wasn't any of those things I'd gifted her with, she was ordinary, not even young, and she had children of her own from a previous marriage. David told her about how his father had treated us, and he didn't pull any punches, but she chose to ignore his words of warning.

She would be taken in by John's lies. And the money, of course. Her head would be well and truly buried in the sand. But finding out I hadn't been replaced by some 'goddess of all things amazing' was good for me; in a way, it set me free. I had fantasised about him being with this wonderful female, blaming myself for not being as perfect as I was convinced she was, telling myself that, if only I'd been like her, John would have been good to me, to us, and he would have respected me, cared for me. We would have been happy. But that was all nonsense, because 'she' was just an idea in my head.

Once the initial anger and frustration had cooled down, I realised that, although this woman was getting the better side of John to begin with, this leopard could never really change his spots. There was no way on earth he could truly alter what was so clearly his basic character.

Of course, getting to this point had taken a lot of counselling, and there was much work to be done. The years had taken their toll and I was at rock bottom. I had actually come to believe that I *was* thick, I *was* a nobody and I deserved *nothing*. I had no confidence, and that was a huge problem, affecting everything I had to do. I would stand in the supermarket aisles in front of rows and rows of jars, packets and tins, dithering about which brand to buy – I couldn't make the simplest decision and I doubted my own judgement on the slightest thing.

I even struggled with my identity, which had been eroded away systematically over years. Who was Paula? What did Paula want? What did she like, dislike, enjoy… what did she think?

So, while John's new life appeared to be playing out happily in front of us, we were still broken and in need of long-term counselling to attempt to repair the deep-rooted damage left in the wake of his campaign of destruction. He didn't need counselling, he wasn't on medication, he never showed any remorse, and he *never, ever said sorry*. He was blameless, of course, and everything was my fault.

For so long, I had hoped that John would see the error of his ways, hoped he would eventually be sorry, feel sorry, say sorry. What I learned was that, in his mind, he had absolutely nothing to be sorry for. He had done nothing wrong.

As I said, it took the first year after the divorce was final, for me to arrive at the belief that the blame for everything didn't fall on me. The one thing I *was* responsible for was not leaving John when he first started showing his true colours, and letting him get away with his evil doings for so long. Yes, I admit that was my fault. And that hurts.

I've dug deep into myself to answer the question, why did I allow it to happen? It's possible to come up with *ideas* for answers, but who can ever know what the real answers are? It's more important to come to terms with the past and move on, however difficult that is. We could all go on asking those same questions forever and a day, and still not know anything.

I racked my brain for such a long time to answer this one, but never really felt I was getting anywhere. Was it because of my childhood? Did the church have too much influence over me? Did I believe too strongly that I always had to conform, to please everyone, to put on an appearance of everything being fine? Or was it because I lost my mum and therefore my family at such a young age, and that left me with a driving need to have a family of my own, and never let them go? Maybe because I left home so young and lost the protection and security of family around me? Or because I married too young and saw that fall apart?

Then there were those other questions I never had answers for. Why was John the person he'd been with us? Was he perhaps a psychopath? What about split personality? Or did he have a narcissistic personality disorder? I studied books and spent many an hour searching around the internet, but – unless you are a qualified professional – that only leads to confusion and even more questions.

Having all of this zapping around in my brain every minute of every day was only adding to my anxiety and stress. Thankfully, the counselling we all received – and still do – has been extremely helpful and has worked wonders for each of us. It has to be said, however, that some of the fallout from our life with that man will probably never leave us, and for that I do beat myself up. A lot.

My Final Chapter: Moving On...

It's just a silly metal plaque, but it made me smile, so I bought it. The picture shows a 1950s mother speaking to her little boy and girl, "Remember, as far as anyone knows, we're a normal family". That was ages ago, when my own children were small, but, over the following years, that image came to represent my own life, with me trying to hide the appalling truth of our existence from family, friends and neighbours. The plaque still hangs in our downstairs cloakroom.

It's a strange experience to look back over the years at a very different life and be able to condense everything that happened into these pages, a bit like recounting a film I saw, but now the children and I are free to live our own life, I can see exactly how it all unfolded.

I know now that the 'Nice John' who pursued me, courted me and wanted us to marry and have a family, was nothing more than a front, a disguise – and, like all disguises, it eventually had to be uncovered.

Although I am in no way qualified to say that John

was a psychopath or a sociopath, or any other label that seems to fit, what I *can* say with absolute conviction is that there is something dreadfully wrong with him, with how his mind works.

There was no way I could possibly have known when we met that I was going to be living a nightmare at the hands of my husband, the father of my children. It all happened over time, in subtle ways, at first just causing me to have questions about John and his odd quirks, but we are all different and unique characters, and surely, tolerating each other's differences has to be a part of a healthy relationship between two people?

The really extreme behaviour only appeared once I was 'under his spell', so deeply entrenched in *being his victim,* another phenomenon now recognised as a condition, known as trauma bonding[2].

That was the period when I would defend John's actions, try to explain them away, when I could see that people around me were wondering why on earth I stayed with him. I believed his promises of better things ahead, time and time again, even though I always ended up being let down and realising that John had lied to me, over and over.

For a long time, I wasted my time and efforts trying to discover what the problem was, so that I could deal with it and – what? – make everything OK? I even considered the most extreme ideas, at one point

---

[2] Trauma Bonding: a biological attachment between victim and abuser in a psychologically abusive relationship

thinking he might be possessed by some 'evil spirit', because at times his behaviour was so unreal, that seemed to be the only explanation. These were the depths to which I sank.

That was then.

Some information from the Office for National Statistics:

It is estimated that 1.9 million adults aged between 16 and 59 were subject to domestic abuse in the year ending March 2017, according to a Crime Survey for England and Wales. This figure is broken down to: 1.2 million women and 713,000 men.

For every 100 domestic abuse-related crimes recorded by 39 police forces in the year ending June 2017, 46 arrests were made.

The majority of domestic homicide victims recorded between April 2013 and March 2016 were females, making up 70% of the total.

There are many excellent organisations out there who are ready and able to help victims of domestic abuse, such as Women's Aid and Refuge, and smaller local organisations offering support, counselling and even accommodation for those in need. In 2017 there were 305 refuge organisations in England and Wales.

My big problem had been that I was terrified of losing my children. Thanks to John's relentless brainwashing, I was convinced they would be taken from me, so I never contacted anyone. Now I know differently, and all I can say is, if you find yourself in a situation where you need help and support, don't make the same mistake. All you have to do is ask.

....

I no longer spend my life thinking about the past; I have far better things to occupy me, starting with David and Alice. We have broken free and we now live life as we want to, making the most of even the simplest activities – like singing and playing music, talking about any subject we choose, spending time with our family, reading books and playing games... ordinary things that other people take for granted, but they give us untold pleasure because we are *free* to do them all now.

One of the saddest outcomes of my years with John was losing my friends, but I know now that this, too, was a part of his need to control, to separate me from everyone I was close to, anyone who could have intervened or exerted some influence when things began to go downhill.

At the time of writing this, I recently met up with Emma, a lady who had been one of my closest friends before my marriage, and it was such a relief to talk openly about everything that had happened, to explain that now I understand I was living in complete denial, controlled in every way by John.

Emma told me that she'd had no option but to abandon our friendship all those years ago – *because John had threatened to kill her husband!* This was a man John had never met, knew nothing about, except the fact that his name was Colin, the same as my dad.

Because Emma had seen me briefly when my teeth were broken and my mobile phone was smashed to bits, she was only too aware that John was capable of bad things. When she and I met that time, I was busy buying a cake for John's birthday, and Emma asked me something I simply couldn't answer.

"Why are you doing that for him when he puts you through such misery?"

I just shook my head.

It took me quite a long time to readjust to 'normal' life and I would find myself feeling shocked at things that had become alien to us, like a family laughing together, children dancing around and giggling at something silly, singing along to the music on the radio and so on. In short, happiness. To us, it had been forbidden.

David and Alice have continued to heal, thank God. Alice eventually went back to university and she thrived there. There is no bond between her and her father, and she doesn't see him very much. David still suffers with anxiety and OCD, the scars of his father's treatment of us all, and I can never forgive myself for that.

As for me, I don't even consider defending John now, and I am truly happy to be free of him. Finally, I have peace of mind, and I am certain that is something he will never know.

I have told my story for different reasons. The first

of these is rather selfish, in that the actual process of putting this book together has become an extremely cathartic experience for me. It's as if transferring the facts, memories and so on from my head on to the pages has allowed me to rid myself of the burden I was carrying around – maybe not completely, but it has certainly helped.

The main reason for my book is that I know my experiences will touch a nerve with many others, whether they are involved in an abusive relationship, or they know someone who is. Hopefully, they will take what happened to me as a caution, something to warn against rushing into a relationship too quickly, to assist in being wary of overlooking or excusing signals that all is not well, and – most importantly – to help those who are in toxic relationships to recognise the need to remove themselves from the dangers of what can only be a worsening situation.

We humans are all very different, individual beings with our own wants and needs, and we all have to deal with life's challenges, its ups and downs, in our own way. But every one of us deserves a happy, healthy life, a life without fear and pain caused by another person, without being controlled by someone through cruelty, threats and violence.

Being unhappy is a waste of human potential, believe me. Every single life is for living, and I now live mine, free of the past.

This is now.

www.ingramcontent.com/pod-product-compliance
Lightning Source LLC
Chambersburg PA
CBHW071225080526
44587CB00013BA/1504